Children's Reflections on Family Life

Children's Reflections on Family Life

Michele Moore
Judith Sixsmith
Kathleen Knowles
with Carolyn Kagan, Suzan Lewis,
Sarah Beazley and Usha Rout

 The Falmer Press
(A member of the Taylor & Francis Group)
London • Washington, D.C.

UK   Falmer Press, 1 Gunpowder Square, London, EC4A 3DE
USA Falmer Press, Taylor & Francis Inc., 1900 Frost Road, Suite 101,
         Bristol, PA 19007

First published in 1996

**A catalogue record for this book is available from the British
Library**

ISBN 0 7507 0573 6 cased
ISBN 0 7507 0574 4 paper

**Library of Congress Cataloging-in-Publication Data are
available on request**

Jacket design by Caroline Archer

Typeset in 10/12 pt, Garamond by
Graphicraft Typesetters Ltd., Hong Kong.

*Printed in Great Britain by Biddles Ltd., Guildford and King's Lynn on
paper which has a specified pH value on final paper manufacture of
not less than 7.5 and is therefore 'acid free'.*

*Every effort has been made to contact copyright holders for their
permission to reprint material in this book. The publishers would be
grateful to hear from any copyright holder who is not here
acknowledged and will undertake to rectify any errors or omissions
in future editions of this book.*

Contents

Contents

Acknowledgments

The original idea for this book arose from discussions at meetings of the Interpersonal and Organisational Development Research Group at the Manchester Metropolitan University's Department of Psychology and Speech Pathology. A debt of gratitude is owed to all the members of this group for their advice, encouragement and practical assistance at the early stages of the book.

Most of all, though, we should like to thank the children whose reflections form the main part of this book for allowing us into their lives; and to their parents and caregivers for their kindness and cooperation with the interviews.

Special thanks go to Marilyn Barnett who undertook the typing of the interview transcripts and juggled all requests to jump the queue with her usual cheerfulness.

Foreword

A book that places at the centre of its analyses what children and young people say is both timely and sorely needed. The discourse of 'listening to children' may have acquired the status of institutional imperative in the form of international child rights legislation, but, as usual, practice tends to lag behind rhetoric. Moreover, with child abuse now gaining increasing public attention, an expertise has emerged around how to talk with, and how to hear, children that threatens to cloud this everyday activity with professional mystery and anxieties about legal implications.

This book presents clear examples and guidance for working with children that make accessible the issues of method and interpretation involved. Rather than waxing polemical or philosophical, it presents its critique of existing work by example. The aim is not to classify or exhaust the range of children's reflections on their family lives, but to exemplify the variation of experience and perception that make generalizations about 'children' and 'families' either patently inappropriate, or so non-specific as to be useless. We read about what children say about the composition of their family — whether this is 'traditional', single-headed, extended beyond the 'nuclear' norm by culture, or extended by caring for elderly or disabled members. Amid a context where children's voices have been omitted or silenced in the policies and practices that structure their lives, research that sets out to explore children's experiences is a welcome departure from the typical work that simply presumes to know what children are, know and need. This book throws such assumptions into question by testifying to the diversity of children's experiences: of where they live, with whom they live. Further, as well as highlighting the diversity of family arrangements, we gain from these chapters a sense of the complexity of the ways the children see themselves and understand how they and their family are seen.

Thus this book joins the emerging body of literature that documents the changing character of childhood and children, and that emphasizes children's active participation in constructing the meanings they live by, and the positions they occupy. The case studies explored are just that: particular instances, of, for example, the family lives of hearing children living with deaf parents, or of children who have crossed national and cultural boundaries to live in Britain. Clearly any of these topics would merit systematic investigation in its own right. But the singularity and specificity of the examples presented in this book are also its strength. These are the diverse but everyday contexts in which everyday children live; so 'normal' and taken for granted as usually to merit attention only when something is considered to have 'gone wrong'. So, typically, the children and families who reach public and professional attention do so within the frame of pathologization. We need to hear about ordinary children's daily lives, to inform and extend our understanding of what 'ordinary' is, and what this means to them. This book starts to do that work of documenting the normalized absence of ordinary children's lives.

The attention to particular, individual 'cases' — whether children or families — serves another purpose too. In these chapters, we see extensive extracts from interviews. One way of reading these is as offering a more direct access to the children's own voices and views, rather than these being submerged within the usual research summary which patronizes by claiming to 'speak for' children. But another way of seeing these is as instances of the process of textualizing the social encounter of talking with children, that is, displaying how an interview is rendered into a text — and thereby making apparent how choices are inevitably made about what parts to reproduce and discuss. Questions of power deeply infuse those of interpretation, not only at the moment of conducting an interview but at every stage in its analysis and commentary.

The authors of this book have been bold and frank in reproducing material here at a level of detail and specificity that is usually obscured from public view, and they make no secret of the dilemmas and difficulties they encountered. As such, it is a valuable resource for parents, professionals and trainers to see how these complex questions of talking, interpreting and writing are negotiated in the context of researching with children.

Erica Burman
February 1996

Chapter 1

Introduction

Michele Moore, Judith Sixsmith and
Kathleen Knowles

What This Book Is About

Despite deeply held notions of the importance of family and home for children, there is wide variation in what children's experiences of family and of home might be. In any discussion about children, their families and their home life, it soon becomes clear that there are many imprecise concepts and hidden assumptions (Alanen, 1992; Burman, 1994). More importantly, the reflections of children themselves on these matters are often overlooked and remain conspicuously absent from the literature. Politicians, parents, journalists, education, health and social services professionals all comment on children's experiences of family life, but children themselves rarely get a say. Leach (1994) suggests that children are the minority group most subject to discrimination and that we are poor at putting children first. Children, with their own experiences, their own desires, needs, thoughts and feelings, are rarely given the opportunity to speak up for themselves. And they are rarely listened to when they do. This means that children's experiences come to be defined in large part by adults. One of the motivations behind this book is to give children an opportunity to present themselves in their own way, giving their views on their home and family life, in order to supplement and amplify the widespread adult representations which typically take centre stage in discussions about children's lives.

In this book, we are not aiming to construct a particular image of what families are, or what families should be, but to illustrate the wide variety of family situations in which children find themselves through their own reflections on their personal situations. Indeed, it very quickly becomes clear that we cannot say what a family or a home is, and the rich variations that children describe provide fascinating insights into these two important concepts. Ideally the book will be used as a resource which, through enabling children to put forward their reflections on family and home, prompts the reader to reflect on their own assumptions and practices that may play a part in shaping children's lives. To this end, throughout the book we have included 'Thinking Points' at the end of each chapter. A range of different strategies are suggested to the reader in these sections: pointers to important issues that have emerged in the chapter; questions that require readers to ponder and reconceptualize if they are willing so to do; and tasks that encourage readers to engage actively with the contents of the chapter. Readers can choose how to make best use of these sections according to individual preference. This emphasis on engaging with the material and reflecting on one's own assumptions and practices is important to us because we firmly believe that if adults make misplaced assumptions about children's lives, then children suffer.

Background

Every Child's Right to be Heard

World-wide discussion on children's rights, and comprehensive argument for a greater respect for children in matters which apply directly to them, provides an important backdrop to this book (Franklin, 1995). In the recent United Nation's Convention on the Rights of the Child, one of the most important rights given to children is the right to be heard (UNICEF, 1995). A child's right to be listened to is viewed as part and parcel of the right to justice for each individual child and for children as a group within society. We feel that children's right to have their reflections taken seriously is part of their entitlement to a full and decent life. It is an intrinsic component of their right to dignity and self-reliance, and fundamental if children's rights to respect and tolerance, and to participation in the life of their own community, are to be realized. Unfortunately, as writers within the UK, we are embroiled in a domestic struggle to achieve such rights for children (Children's Rights Office, 1995). At the time of writing, for example, our government continues to militate against international standards by elevating parental choice over children's rights (Newell, 1995). As a society, we may feel we have a duty to look to children's best interests, but without prioritizing their own viewpoints and concerns we have little hope of recognizing their rights.

Historically, the acceptance of children's experiential knowledge about their lives as meaningful knowledge has presented adults with difficulties. In this book, we propose that a fresh approach is needed to make children's reflections visible, particularly in academic domains. Consequently, we have worked hard to provide the children taking part in the project with innovative means of engaging with the research process. We are committed to taking children's views seriously within research, and to giving them as much control as possible over what they say, how they say it and what we do with what they say. We argue that it is incumbent upon adults to ensure *all* children are able to make their views known, irrespective of age or maturity, communication strategy or impairment. Hence the book includes the reflections of very young children as well as their more mature peers, of children with impairments as well as their non-disabled peers, of girls and of boys, and of children from a variety of cultural and linguistic minority groups. However, at this point we should point out one considerable gap: we have not accessed the views of children who communicate without spoken language. We did have provision for children using British Sign Language to take part. But children who communicate without a recognize oral/aural or manual/visual language were excluded from this study, and we would agree with Micheline Mason (1995) that for this group of children, researchers must redouble their efforts to guarantee both their inclusion in research, and representation of their views, as a matter of urgency.

Thus, albeit with some limitations, this book is about the importance of placing children's views at the front of policies and practices which impact on their family lives. It requires the reader to accept that children are knowledgable, so that we can look again at family and home matters afresh, from children's own viewpoints.

Debates About the Family

The family, in its many different forms, is constantly in the forefront of public debate. Discussions about family structures and processes — such as the merits of single-parent-headed versus two parent families, the economic role of fathers and the role of the Child Support Agency, gay parenthood and issues of fertility and infertility — are informed by adult beliefs and ideologies, but children themselves also have an important perspective. Children are recognized as an integral part of family life but internal power structures often relegate them to the bottom of a family hierarchy. Yet children are a vital part of the adult world, they play a part which deserves respect as 'present participants in, and future heirs to, adult affairs' (Leach, 1994, p.7). It might even be said that families do not exist *for* children but *because* of them.

Throughout the book we are able to show how children actively construct their everyday life in relation to some of these issues. What emerges is that their responses are not predictable. Living in a certain type of family does not imply a certain kind of childhood. As has been noted elsewhere, 'there are many childhoods and children, too, participate significantly in their making' (Alanen, 1992, p.131).

This book seeks to promote understanding of a wide range of family types (Fine, 1993). However, not all different family structures can be addressed within the pages of this book: we are aware that important dimensions of family diversity are not represented here, such as multi-generational families, families in which parental death has occurred, and families located within the drug culture. These are all equally as deserving of our attention. We hope that by exposing both common themes and critical differences between diverse family types we can give the readers a feeling for the legitimacy of listening to children's experiences from whatever family background they emerge. Our starting point is that children's reflections on family lives are worthy of study in their own right and not just in relation to adult perspectives.

At this juncture it is appropriate to acknowledge that even to talk in terms of diverse family types is almost to assume that each 'family type' is in some way consistent. Our intention is not to make such an assumption. Families exist and operate within their own context of socially constructed meanings. Each family is an integral whole, with its own culture, value systems and so on. The notion of 'family types' is used here simply as a descriptive and orienting term to cover an elaborate complexity of family realities.

When we began pulling children's stories together, we discovered a number of recurrent issues and themes. These include the value of gathering information from children, the need for children to have a voice, the importance of recognizing pressures and stressors in children's lives and the necessity for identifying coping strategies that go beyond the capabilities of individual members of the families. These topics will be encountered throughout the book, together with debates about the nature of both family and childhood and the way in which they are socially and historically constructed and personally experienced (Ingelby, 1986; Alanen, 1992; Burman, 1994).

How We Developed This Project

We came together as a group of seven women with expertise in different areas of psychology and speech pathology but a shared interest in children and their views on family life. The particular family contexts we have selected reflect our research and professional interests as well as our experience in families; all of us as children, most of us as parents. We recognize, as has already been explained, that inevitably we have not considered all the different family forms in which children are growing up. Nevertheless, what emerges is a picture of children's experiences of family lives which questions assumptions about 'the family' as one ideal form.

The content of each chapter emerges from many hours of talking with children. As exemplified by the 'Thinking Points', we have all tried to link what children say in their accounts to real issues for professionals and parents who might be prompted to rethink aspects of their own ways of reacting to and dealing with children in families.

Methodological Issues

The Children Who Took Part

Twenty children took part in our project. They represented a wide age range, from the youngest who was 5 years old to the eldest at 17. Each child contributed as fully as they could to the research process. In accordance with our project aims, the children were living in a variety of family situations, including children belonging to cultural and linguistic minority groups, children with impairments, those with gay parents, adoptive parents and so on. Some of the children belonged to large family groups, with many brothers and sisters, others were the 'only' children of the family. We also aimed to make sure that both boys and girls took part in the study, although more boys were eventually interviewed than girls (fourteen boys and six girls).

We contacted our participants through personal networks and each child is introduced in the chapter to which they contribute. It must be noted here that while each child was interviewed in relation to their predominant family structure, all families are complex entities and the arbitrary classifications we have constructed for this book are not mutually exclusive. For example, a child interviewed because of their Asian family background might just as easily have been included in the dual career family chapter since both parents pursued careers.

The total number of children taking part is small (twenty), and we do not make any claims that the sample is likely to be representative. Nevertheless, we consider that the material presented highlights sufficiently wide-ranging issues for it to be applicable to a great many children and their families. We realize, however, that many academics and most policy-makers remain firmly attached to the fantasy of collecting 'objective' data and may be reluctant to accept ways in which the research reported here has benefited, we think enormously, by distance from the illusion of objective data collection. We are happy to admit that the information we present simply gives rise to one particular way of seeing things. Critics may question whether we have presented 'the real picture', but we will argue that this does not actually matter. The most important aim has been to prompt readers to challenge their own way of looking at children's experiences of family life. We do not deny that we have our own motivations for presenting issues in a particular way, but we hope we have prioritized what children themselves have had to say for this book to consist, as far as possible, in the reflections they were interested in.

So far as possible, the children's stories are allowed to tell themselves with minimal incursion by the writer on the reader's response, and this makes them very powerful. However, we are aware that their reflections have come about within the research situation and have been filtered through our own perspectives and interpretations (Henwood and Pidgeon, 1995). Indeed, the children's material has been presented either in case-study or thematic form depending on who was interviewed and what information was gained. Furthermore, the chapters represent only a partial account of the children's experiences in terms of what the children wanted to reveal to us from the particular point in time at which the research took place. Nevertheless, the whole research enterprise undertaken here was one which sought to reveal the children's experiences in as holistic a way as possible. Each child's story casts a unique light on family life, conveying children's realities, and confirming that the subjectivity and power of children's voices is incredibly important for anyone interested in making sense of their lives.

How We Interviewed the Children

The predicaments faced by children in a variety of circumstances have been elicited through interviews in which we utilized a variety of strategies for helping children to recall and describe those aspects of their family life which they chose to share. Pilot interviews soon revealed that even the most open-ended form of semi-structured interview (Denzin and Lincoln, 1994) did not always adequately allow children free expression. It was extremely difficult to reveal the children's subjectivities (Henwood and Nicholson, 1995). Some of the younger children felt slightly intimidated by the interview situation and were keen to get the answers 'right' to help the researcher do their job. Also, some children struggled to articulate their feelings and experiences in a way which would make sense both to themselves and the researcher. We needed to encourage the children to take the lead in expressing their own experiences and concerns, and to take the time to allow them to find a comfortable medium of communication through play and talk. Consequently it was necessary to take a highly humanistic and reflexive approach to the research (Bowman, Bowman and Resch, 1984; Shakespeare, Atkinson and French, 1993; Moore, et al, forthcoming).

Eventually, the interviews centred around methodological techniques such as the construction of the child's family tree, drawings of their family and sets of key questions aimed at enabling the children to recount their experiences as part of an ongoing conversation with the researchers. Throughout the interviews, researchers were careful to reinforce the notion of the child as expert of their own experiences. While the interview concentrated on children's thoughts about family life, any emotional issues that these raised for the child were dealt with sensitively, and we did, of course, abide by the ethical principles for conducting research with child participants as laid down by our respective professional bodies. However, it is important to recognize that interviewing children did present researchers with wide-ranging dilemmas and some of these are briefly considered next.

Difficulties in Interviewing Children for Research

It was with some trepidation that we began to task of interviewing children. It had seemed like a very worthwhile idea during one summer afternoon meeting; to try to uncover children's own reflections of their home and family lives. After all, as we have pointed out, it isn't very often that children's thoughts and opinions are heard clearly and taken seriously, particularly in a domain as private and all-embracing as home and family life. We had affirmed our commitment to respecting children's rights to have their say taken seriously. Then doubts began to creep in about the enormity of the task.

As already explained, we contacted the children via our own families, friends and acquaintances. As soon as we were each faced with the prospect of an impending interview, our doubts concerning our personal skills for enabling children to talk about their experiences of family life began to surface. We took advice about helping children recall from other researchers (Cronin, 1993) but knew there could be no cookbook approach to conducting such sensitive interviews. Several dilemmas need to be considered here.

Even though we had mediated access to the children through personal contacts, we were often relative strangers to them and complicated boundaries issues quickly became apparent. We all felt that we needed to explain the process and aims of the research carefully to the children and to converse in a language which children could readily understand. Our aim was to put the children at ease so that they could enjoy the interviews, but this was a more complex business than we had at first imagined. We were soon reminded that children are very skilled at putting adults at ease and, moreover, sufficiently competent at doing this to often mask the extent to which they are actually at ease themselves. One possibility for researchers is to talk about themselves and their own family to help the child feel comfortable about sharing reflections. The difficulty with this lies in the shaping effect that this may have on the child. Similarly, strategies are needed to show recognition of children's own tactics for managing difficulties in the interview process: recognizing when 'I don't know' means 'I don't want to say' or 'I don't know how to say', for example. All this meant that, as well as interviewing, we had continually to be observing and interpreting the children's responses and in retrospect we would say that when interviewing children there is no substitute for being able to anticipate the intensive effort required in respect of these issues. With very young children, we found the advantages of interviewing in pairs inestimable.

The children wanted to know what was 'research'? What was an 'interview'? Why had we chosen to talk to them? What would happen during the interview? And afterwards, what would happen with the tape-recording of their words? What about the other children we would talk to, what were they like? Who would we tell what they had said? Could they tell secrets? Could we keep secrets? And so on. We quickly realized that we could not cast ourselves in the conventional role of interviewers who know what it is useful to discuss and find out. It was much more important to let children choose their own agendas, following their lead in to a focus on family and home.

The complexities of 'confidential' versus 'anonymous' and 'private' versus 'secret' contributions raised tremendous dilemmas in this research. To avoid some of the obvious pitfalls we explained to each child that we would give them a pretend name in our book. We emphasized, 'You can tell anyone you like about what we say. I will keep what you say private, but you can choose to tell other people if you want.' But these strategies do not, of course, avoid potential conflict between a child and a parent if they can be recognized in the text. We decided to exclude data if a child indicated that it was not for public airing, 'You won't tell anyone that will you?': though this was never easy to determine and often resulted in partial accounts becoming even more partial. We can ensure anonymity from the general readership, in terms of what the children say and how we report it, however, we cannot ensure anonymity from parents and other family members if we give too much personal detail for any child. Chapter writers have independently decided upon how much detail to provide. We have dealt with these issues to the best of our abilities, but are mindful that they are not fully resolved in this book. All children in the book have been given pseudonyms and names of other people they mentioned, or places talked about, are changed too.

Most of the sessions were tape-recorded (where the agreement of the children and their parents or caregivers was given) and the tapes were subsequently transcribed. Detailed notes were taken when tape-recording was not possible. These processes gave rise to the tensions surrounding power and control which inevitably face researchers who interview children. How to ensure parents remain as near as the child wants them, but are not intrusive. Who 'owns' the transcript? A young child, who may not yet be literate? Or do researchers, or parents, own the transcript? Does a parent (any parent in particular?) have a right to read their child's transcript? We feel we made only partial headway so far as finding a resolution for these dilemmas goes, which is why it has been important at least to disclose our concerns.

Given the many debates and conflicts which characterize research interviews with children, a further intention of this book is to map out some of the ways in which these issues manifest themselves in practice.

Why We Wrote This Book

The aims of the book can be summarized as follows:

- To demonstrate the importance, through presenting what children have to say for themselves, of placing children's reflections firmly at the front of policy and practice that claim to be about improving their family situations.
- To illustrate the variety of positions in which children find themselves — with chapters drawing on different issues in family life, including dual career families, families with multiple commitments, split-families, families with disabled parents, culturally diverse and transnational families, as well as traditional family situations.
- To provide practical insights for families and professionals based on what children say about the complexities of modern family life.
- To set an agenda for future discussion of approaches to both children and policy which aim to be family-friendly in the fullest sense. It has become fashionable to consider the implementation of 'family-friendly' policies and for policy-makers to purport to develop policies

designed to 'strengthen the family'. Any consultations underpinning these developments, however, rarely, if ever, include children's perspectives and we have sought to redress this imbalance.

How This Book is Organized

We have arranged the children's accounts to focus on the whole experience that they chose to talk about, in preference to sorting out patterns relating to any particular stages of their lives. This format leaves the nitty-gritty of children's concerns intact, and shows clearly how children are actively involved in the construction of their own family lives, rather than being passive recipients of family structure (James and Prout, 1990). By adopting this experiential approach, readers can easily immerse themselves in stories which connect with their own immediate interests.

Each chapter takes a real concern that children find themselves confronting within their family lives and draws on children's reflections to illustrate the reasons why, and the ways in which, professionals may wish to reconsider some of their everyday assumptions and practices.

In the first chapter, Judith Sixsmith and Kathleen Knowles present children's views of the traditional nuclear family. The increasingly elusive traditional family is tracked down, in which both parents are the child's biological parents, the adult female takes major responsibility for caring, and the adult male fulfils the role of provider. The pros and cons of this most conventional model of family life become clear through the reflections of children whose hopes, dreams and anxieties are found not to be so far removed from those of their peers in less customary situations.

In the second chapter, Suzan Lewis and co-authors review the situation of children whose parents both pursue demanding careers. The difficulties as well as the advantages of this type of family life are revealed. It is evident that, in some circumstances, stress experienced by dual career parents may spill over to create stressful home environments for children, but that the careful negotiation of roles within the family can reduce the impact of these pressures on children and enhance the potential benefits of this family context.

The chapter by Carolyn Kagan and Suzan Lewis, on families with multiple commitments, focuses on the experiences of children in families where different family responsibilities — for employment, young children, elderly relatives and so on — have to be managed, sometimes in unsupportive contexts. The children reveal a range of different personal coping strategies that they have developed, and these are considered in relation to adequate support that could be provided.

Michele Moore and Sarah Beazley consider children's responses to their situation when parents live apart. Their perspective on topical debates concerning split family life is explored. Myths about the disadvantages when parents are separated are challenged as the children are able to consider positive aspects of their circumstances which contrast with negative images of dependency and insufficiency which currently abound in the mass media.

In the next chapter, Sarah Beazley and Michele Moore explore the reflections of children who have Deaf parents. Children whose parents are disabled are frequently viewed either as martyrs or victims. However, the reflections in this chapter reveal that children with disabled parents are no more virtuous or unfortunate than their non-disabled peers, but the social and material environment in which the family find itself can be profoundly disabling and this has a greater impact on the children than the impairment which their parents have.

Usha Rout and co-authors discuss culturally diverse families. Children talk about their experiences as members of families that are characterized by cultural diversity and the reader will find interesting overlaps with issues raised by other chapters. The advantages and disadvantages of experiencing a range of cultural influences are explored and presented through the children's words. Recommendations are made for how children might be encouraged to withstand conflicting pressures and positively cope with diversity.

In the eighth chapter, Kathleen Knowles and Judith Sixsmith describe the situation of children in transnational families. The free movement of workers between member states of the European Community is one factor behind the growing situation in which children live with their family in one country and then move with their family to another. The impact of such a move is explored through the interviews presented in this chapter. Accounts given by the children reaffirm the importance of providing children with practical strategies for coping with the potential stresses of culture shock. Children's emotional well-being, educational progress and peer relations are seen to merit special attention as children try to assimilate the changes.

The final chapter reviews issues raised by the children and draws attention to developing innovative ways for responding to children in the variety of circumstances in which they find themselves. Recommendations are made for how both individual children, and the whole family, can be empowered to withstand adversity and positively cope with stress. We consider the role of family-friendly policies which may help to maximize children's assorted experiences of family circumstances. Practical ideas to maximize children's experiences of family life are discussed. The common and most critical thread in all of the chapters is the celebration of children's subjective accounts.

We have set out to challenge stereotypical assumptions which are often made about the position of children in different family contexts. We have found that there are many lessons to be learned from children's reflections. Hopefully our book will widen and stimulate discussion which will lead to the development of children and family-friendly policy and practice. There is a need for children to be placed firmly in the driving seat when decisions are made which claim to be in their best interests. The children's perspectives presented in this book provide notable testimony to this. The book brings a new significance to realizing the concerns of children and, at the same time, links together the reflections of children who experience a wide range of family circumstances.

Note

To assist the reader we would like to clarify that, in quotations, two dots (. .) indicate that the speaker pauses, and three dots (. . .) indicate that material has been left out.

Thinking Points

- Before reading on, it will be useful to bring to mind your own assumptions about and images of a family. Draw a picture of your own family — a match-stick drawing will suffice. On one side of the picture note anything that occurs to you about how your family is similar to other families you know. On the other side, note anything about how your family is different from other families with whom you are familiar. Compare your own family to any other. Do the similarities or differences matter? If so, how and why?

- Take a look at popular representations of families; for example, in newspapers and magazines, in charity advertisements, images in films, on television and so on. What messages come across about what a family is? How are children portrayed? How are parents represented? What are the implications of viewing families in these ways? Are there more enabling ways in which families could be depicted?

- What do you think a family is? Try to sketch out your personal view on what the key characteristics of a family are. What are the essential ingredients of 'a family'? What are the essential ingredients of 'home'? How do you know?

Chapter 2

Home Life in the 'Traditional Family'

Judith Sixsmith and Kathleen Knowles

Introduction

When we began to undertake research for this book, we felt it was important that children from 'traditional families' were represented. All too often it is assumed that the 'traditional family' is the ideal type of family and that children brought up within them experience a stable, fulfilling and enjoyable childhood. An excerpt from the *Observer* illustrates the predominance in public consciousness of the 'traditional family' structures as an ideal, '. . . two committed parents provide a child with the best chance of survival, and . . . children need the stability and security of that relationship' (*Observer*, 17 October 1993). The fact that traditional families are not a homogeneous phenomenon and that such children live through a variety of experiences (some adverse, some not) can sometimes be forgotten (White and Woollett, 1992). It is worth remembering that families constitute different environments for different family members at different points in the family lifecycle (Burman, 1994). As such, children in traditional families deserve a voice in our society (Franklin, 1995; Leach, 1994) alongside those children whose circumstances are perhaps more obviously disadvantaged. It was with this in mind that children's reflections of traditional family life were sought.

But what exactly is a 'traditional family'? Families vary enormously in their structure, emotional atmosphere and organization (Dilworth-Anderson, Burton and Turner, 1993). How were we to identify 'traditional families' for the purposes of the research? Politicians, researchers and the media tend to define it as a white, biologically related, nuclear family with children, headed by a heterosexual couple, in which fathers are breadwinners and mother are fulltime caretakers (White and Woollett, 1992; Fine, 1993). This definition seemed to be fairly parsimonious, so, armed with these basic (but in some ways, hopelessly inadequate) criteria, we could begin to identify suitable families.

However, we quickly realized that the 'traditional family' is almost as difficult to find as it is to define. In our increasingly multicultural society, family stability is threatened as the divorce rate rises (in 1990, 3.2 divorces granted per 1000 people: Leach, 1994), and single parent \ step families are created. The existence of the traditional family has been further eroded as more and more women have entered the workforce out of financial necessity or through career (as well as family) orientation (Lewis and Knowles, 1995).

After contacting a number of friends, we eventually found four families who fitted the 'traditional family' criteria and whose children were willing to take part in the research. Two pilot interviews were conducted which prepared us for the task of talking with children about their private family experiences. In the pilot interviews we learned that the confines of formal interviewing were not particularly helpful when revealing young children's reflections on their everyday family life. It was important to avoid a situation in which the children felt they had to supply the 'right' answers to set questions. It was more appropriate to spend time with them, to play and talk with them in a natural way and on their own terms. The interaction between us was better structured by the children's concerns and interests, but there was a hidden agenda (Harre and Secord, 1972) of issues that we introduced into our conversations when appropriate. In this way it was possible to proceed with the research, listening carefully to the children, asking them questions and enabling their voices to emerge through our joint time spent together. Judith Sixsmith took responsibility for interviewing the children whose accounts are central to this chapter.

It was at this point that the research proper began with two boys, Adam and Jason. Judith had never met either boy before nor had she met their families. In accordance with the aim to understand children's experiences within 'traditional family' units, both boys were white and lived with their biological parents. The fathers were employed in daytime jobs and the mothers worked at home as housewives.

The boys' experiences are described below, although it must be borne in mind that the interviews gained only a partial view of their highly complex family life. The descriptions are presented as two separate case studies. We use the word 'descriptions' since we want to give voice to the children's experiences rather than over-indulge in researcher interpretations. Consequently, much of the material is in the form of quotations taken from the interviews. We have presented the data as case studies as this helps to preserve, as far as possible, the child's story and its perspective intact.

Children's Reflections

Jonathan

At the time of interview, Jonathan was 'nearly 13'. He was a confident child and very much at home with the research situation. His outgoing personality was evident in his easy ability to chat with a stranger. Jonathan had been looking forward to the interview all day. His curiosity about the purpose of the session was quickly satisfied, and Judith and he slipped comfortably into a flowing conversational style.

Jonathan was the only child of Andrew (aged 45) and Sharon (40ish). They lived in a three bedroomed semi on a quiet street in a medium-sized town in Merseyside, with a pet budgie. Andrew worked as a college lecturer. Getting to work involved a half hour car journey, morning and evening. In the evenings, Andrew arrived at home between six and seven o'clock. Jonathan had joined a new secondary school in the previous autumn term. He had settled well into the school and made friends there. Sometimes, in the mornings, Andrew would drive Jonathan to school, usually after a late lie in and a rushed breakfast.

In addition to his parents, Jonathan's extended family included his four grandparents, an uncle, aunty and two cousins. Although he did not have a great deal of contact with his mum's parents (living in the South of England), Jonathan did see his dad's parents and uncle's family regularly. Jonathan enjoyed the weekly visits to his grandparent's house and would play with his younger cousins there. This gave him a sense of being part of a much larger family unit. He enjoyed these play sessions as he missed not having brothers or sisters of his own. Being an only child was a source of much contemplation for Jonathan. Thinking about his own family situation, he concluded:

> Being an only one, you know, it's got its advantages but, on balance,
> I would definitely have two kids, because I know how I feel. Yeah,
> I think the best would be about three and I wouldn't like to see their
> lives to be torture of doing the chores, you see. I'd lay a few ground
> rules down like, be home before ten, that sort of thing, like that.

Although Jonathan intimated that he sometimes felt lonely through the lack of brothers or sisters, he never explicitly articulated this feeling. Perhaps this might be accounted for by understanding how Jonathan perceived his family context. Family life was, for Jonathan, not just a matter of himself and his parents. It included his wider family, friends and pets. Perhaps the most interesting conception of family life for Jonathan was the notion of the integral link between people sharing their lives together:

> *Interviewer*: Right now Jonathan, tell me all the words that come into
> your head when you think of the word 'family'.
> *Jonathan*: Parents, pets, relatives, friends, juggling . . sharing.
> *Interviewer*: Sharing?
> *Jonathan*: I mean you have people around you, being comfortable,
> living their lives together [in] a place where you belong.

Jonathan talked about the way in which the sharing of family life was made possible through the physical locus and constancy of his home:

> Sharing like that, you have to have a home there, a roof, your own
> room, the people in it. It's warm. A place to belong to. That's the best
> way to describe it. So you can all be together in one place.

In his spare time, Jonathan had developed a wide range of hobbies and interests centred around his family and home. In addition to cycling, playing guitar and cooking, Jonathan said:

I like basketball, skateboarding, juggling, unicycling, art, sciences, history, geography and most other subjects, but not maths.

He enjoyed sharing these interests with friends, but also with his father. Jonathan's relationship with his father seemed to be warm and close. When asked to describe his dad, Jonathan was enthusiastic in reply:

Jonathan: He's all right actually. He's fun, but at times his work does take over.
Interviewer: Tell me about the fun bit to start off with.
Jonathan: The fun bit, well we used to go cycling, but now we don't have the bike, because he sold it. He sort of like would start . . but when we did it was fun because he knows like Texas or MFI, but we know whether we could go over hills and, well, over mounds of rubble there is this sort of a steep hill and we go down that.
Interviewer: So it's fun.
Jonathan: Yeah, exciting, turn round you know and you don't want to leave there, because you can ride up and you can sort of like pull a skid. Well, you can like stop your bike, your bike goes right round, and you set off but trying to just put your wheel on the floor about that much before you can go down, and you sort of drop like a bit and it sort of goes like that and goes steeper and then you sort of have a little bit of a jump.

The excitement of cycling with his father was complemented by quieter games:

We play that [French Cricket] and if we do I don't want to go inside you know. I want to keep doing it. I want to beat him because he usually beats me, apart from the odd time.

and musical interests:

Jonathan: We play the guitars. I play them, so does dad. That's a homemade guitar, made by dad and me.
Interviewer: Is it?
Jonathan: Yeah, it works apart from the middle pick up. Dad plays the bass, I play guitar.
Interviewer: Do you play together?
Jonathan: We play the guitars together, yeah, and the guitar and bass together, yeah. I like doing Chuck Berry and Buddy Holly and stuff.
Interviewer: Do you do that in the evenings or weekends?

> *Jonathan*: We do that in the evenings, whenever we can really. I mean we were watching Glastonbury together, on Saturday night and I didn't go to bed until half eleven or so.

Jonathan's father was also the person most likely to help him out with his homework:

> Well, my dad does [helps with homework], but it depends on if it's really difficult maths which it never is, but if there is a sort of a question I get stuck on, a trick question, I either ask my mum and if she doesn't know, my dad does. My dad explains it to me, not telling me the answer. I sort of like work to the answer with my dad helping me.

Sometimes Andrew would need to stay late at work and other times he would bring work home after finishing his college day. Jonathan had little idea what his father's work actually involved, but he was aware that his dad would need space at home to fulfil his work commitments:

> *Interviewer*: You were talking about your dad, you said he was fun but sometimes work gets in the way. Can you tell me about that?
> *Jonathan*: Well, like a couple of days ago he had papers, I think, yeah. It was a bit before the show [art show at college] he had papers and was sort of like there sitting doing all the reports and sort of like I have to stay out of the room, you know, so he can concentrate. Don't know how he does it. Like I say I prefer being with people.
> *Interviewer*: So he teaches?
> *Jonathan*: He's a lecturer and teacher of silver something, graphics, well graphics silver something.

Contact with his father was further limited by Andrew's nights out with friends:

> *Jonathan*: He's got a couple of friends who come around and they go to the pub, right, sometimes. But if, I mean, we don't see a lot of him, but there was a TV thing saying that some fathers only see 37 seconds of their kids everyday. So on that basis [I] see him quite a lot really. But if sort of like half an hour a day, something like that I'd say, I'd see him not a lot, but quite a bit.
> *Interviewer*: Would you like to see more of him?
> *Jonathan*: Yeah. It's just the hours he works, you know, and school, which provides me with two hours free when I get home to do my homework.

While Jonathan would have enjoyed spending more time with his dad, he seemed to understand that work commitments were important and that this meant less time together. He did appreciate the quality time his dad gave him and their relationship appeared, from Jonathan's perspective, to be stable and fulfilling.

Jonathan was less able to discuss his relationship with his mum since it was based less on sharing activities and more on the routines, everyday cares and concerns of family life:

> *Interviewer*: What about your mum? What's she like?
> *Jonathan*: Irritating at times. Well, it really depends you know on the circumstances that you're in. Like if I come in and I've got homework, like, I usually do it on the kitchen table. But now I've been told, like warned, not to do it on the kitchen table, to go upstairs and do it on the bed.
> *Interviewer*: You don't like that as much?
> *Jonathan*: No, because I have somebody to talk to. Well, I can do it if I've got people around me I can actually do it. But if I'm on my own, I just lose my concentration.
> *Interviewer*: Why do you like people around?
> *Jonathan*: I don't know, it's just sort of like not being helpless if I get stuck on a question or something. Somebody's there to help me, you know.

Cooking and art were activities which Jonathan enjoyed sharing with his mum:

> *Interviewer*: What kinds of things do you do with your mum?
> *Jonathan*: Cook. I like cooking, yeah. Not many boys do, but I do. I've made sponge cakes, chocolate cakes all the things that are bad for you but taste really nice. I mean, I've made meals. I've made scrambled eggs, all the dead simple stuff. I know all that off by heart.
> *Interviewer*: What else do you do with your mum?
> *Jonathan*: Art. She helps me draw and stuff like that. I can get all the points, you know sort of, like vanishing points. I learned it at school and then I forgot it and then mum taught me it, and so did dad.

Jonathan's lack of detailed knowledge of his dad's job was echoed by his lack of knowledge of his mum's daytime routine:

> I'm at school, yeah, but I mean sometimes she goes to Ikea with my friend's mum Cath, and then they'll come back for coffee. She'll have coffee mornings at friends' houses, like that. The only thing that I do know that she definitely does is, when I go to school, sit down and have a cup of tea . . and gets on with the chores.

Nevertheless, family life was well structured by routines concerning getting up in the morning, eating and going to bed. Jonathan had learned to respect the value of a well-ordered family life. Jonathan and his dad played a minor role in daily household routines, rarely contributing to the housework. Household chores were, for them, largely reserved for special occasions:

> I do it on special occasions. I have been known to do it myself without being asked, like if it's my birthday or something, it's sort of an honorary rest. Or if it's mum's birthday, I'll make breakfast. Mother's day, yeah. Father's day, yeah.

Everyday routines were punctuated by family rituals surrounding special events such as Saints' days, Christmas and birthdays, which Jonathan found both fun and comforting. Such rituals confirmed to Jonathan his place in a well-understood and caring family environment:

> *Interviewer*: All right, and what's your dad called?
> *Jonathan*: Andrew.
> *Interviewer*: and how old is he?
> *Jonathan*: 45.
> *Interviewer*: Sounds pretty firm. Has he had a birthday?
> *Jonathan*: No, I only know from the envelopes that my dad does.
> *Interviewer*: From the?
> *Jonathan*: From the envelopes that my mum and dad send each other. They sort of put cards and put them on the floor of the porch, you see. And my dad, when it's my mum's birthday, he does the age on the back and colours it in, sort of the night before, half past ten, sitting in bed trying to colour this thing. I put mine under my bed and my dad gets up early and puts it outside.

This stable family background gave Jonathan the potential to cope with new and disruptive situations. For instance, the prospect of his mum going out to work did not unduly worry Jonathan. He felt he could manage any difficulties himself since he was growing up and becoming more independent of his parents:

> If mum was working full time I'd give her credit you know, because it's hard to get a job. Just depends on what it is though. It really depends because you really have to get used to it though. I mean I'm used to this way, my mum not working. I'd just get used to another routine. I mean the only thing, I would feel lonely coming home, and there would be no-one, absolutely deserted. The only thing I would like about it is the keys to the house.

As a 12-year-old, Jonathan had developed a way of life which integrally involved both his family and friends. His budding independence was perhaps best articulated in his description of a rather full social and educational life outside of the immediate family. Once a week he had maths, English and guitar lessons but his main interest lay in becoming a performer or entertainer:

> *Jonathan*: I go juggling on Saturday. In Taunton, not so far from our school actually. For about three hours for a pound.
> *Interviewer*: So are you entertaining people or learning?
> *Jonathan*: No, we're learning. It's sort of like go every Saturday and you don't turn up if you don't want to. It's really fun, actually. I mean we have races. What we do, we put two chairs out or three chairs and what we have to do is weave in and out on the inside course, you see. Or we used to play like unicycle gladiators and you used to go round like that, spin the wheel twice and try and push each other off the unicycle . . entertaining . . that's all I want to do apart from throwing cocktails.

Friends also formed an important part of Jonathan's social life; organized around shared activities such as fixing up his old bike and visiting each other's houses to play on the computer. Jonathan had a number of friends at school, and some living in his street who he often played with outside of school hours:

> I did get a bike for nothing, an old bike, and I'm doing that up. I'm doing it up myself with a friend, my dad's helping . . it's enjoyable.

> When my friends and I go out playing football, I mean, that's the only thing he ever likes. But you see, I sort of like go out to join him. I sort of like go in goal you know. I'm the street's goalie.

Increasing independence did not mean, however, increasing alienation from home life. Jonathan always related his everyday experiences to his family and home. When describing his recent exam successes, he clearly valued the pride that his parents expressed, even though at times it could be embarrassing:

> *Jonathan*: I did exceptionally well in music, yeah, 81 per cent, my highest mark. I got top marks for chemistry and they [parents] were proud of me for that.
> *Interviewer*: How did you know?
> *Jonathan*: You can't really explain it, you just know because there is all of this like keep talking about it. All this conversation and if my parents keep talking, you know that they're proud. Like when people come round and you're sitting at one end of the table, and thinking, 'Oh no, please no. I'm sure you don't want to listen to this,' so you think, 'Stop talking,' ready to strangle them.

As intimated above, family life was not always smooth running and Jonathan complained at times:

> *Jonathan*: I don't like my family with the aggravating times you get sometimes.
> *Interviewer*: When are the aggravating times?
> *Jonathan*: When you're having your room decorated. It's clear out of the way before the trouble starts. But what I really don't like about my family is the chores. I mean, everybody says this but I've sort of like got a phobia of chores, I don't like them, won't do them.
> *Interviewer*: What sort of chores do you do?
> *Jonathan*: Stacking the dishwasher, cleaning him out [the budgie], doing his water and seed every day, and then you have to disinfect the cage.

Discipline within the household was fairly relaxed, although Jonathan was keenly aware of family rules about his behaviour and what the consequences were for misbehaving:

> *Interviewer*: What happens when you've done something naughty?
> *Jonathan*: That's a strange thing, 'trouble'. I don't get in trouble much
> . . yeah, it's a sort of waiting for the storm to come . . you know when that cold feeling goes up the middle of your body and you're sort of like, 'Sorry, sorry, sorry, sorry', apologizing every minute and mum goes, 'OK you admit it', you know, and tells me off and all that lot.

Indeed, there was a strong sense of the family moral code which he was comfortable with:

> *Interviewer*: In your family, what are the things that are right, and what's the wrong things to do?
> *Jonathan*: Stealing, taking cash. The only time we ever take cash is if we find it on the floor, you know in the house. Everything is wrong if it's smashing up things or breaking the law, apart from going over the speed limit. I mean, we often do that to get me to school on time
> . . the maximum we've done over the speed limit on the dual carriage-way is about ten, you know, but that ten gets us there three minutes quicker.
> *Interviewer*: And what's right?
> *Jonathan*: You can't really say what's right because you are doing right things all the time. You must speak your mind, even if you don't know what you're doing, you just speak it. You speak what you want, what you believe in, what should be done, but that's the only problem, your mind just goes out of control because sometimes you've had it. You can upset people that way.

Although Jonathan was a cheerful boy with a strong sense of his own personality and his own family life, he told about times when he felt upset and needed advice and guidance. For example, on one occasion he talked of being bullied at school and on another he reported an incident with a drunken, threatening man while he shopped with his friend in the town centre. In these cases, Jonathan knew his parents, particularly his mum, were there to help:

> *Jonathan*: I'm just so insecure on my own. Someone was bashing me around at Allan High [school] so I hit him because nobody would stand up to him. But I know that I could actually defend myself if I had to, but I just feel safer in a group. This guy came up to us who had been drinking came up to us and said, 'Do you know how to defend yourself?' and all that, you know .. and he stood there for about half an hour, and I'm going, 'Oh no, I don't know what I'm going to do here.' You don't know what to do, whether to do something right or wrong here.
>
> *Interviewer*: If you got upset about something, who would you talk to?
>
> *Jonathan*: I would probably talk to my mum actually, or failing that, I would probably talk to my friend across the road. But there are some things I wouldn't talk to my dad about, about girlfriends. It's too embarrassing.

Jonathan had a reasonably well-developed support network structured around his mum and friends. He was fully aware of his place in the family structure, a cherished only child whose main contribution to the family was to be happy, do well at school and care for others. He always knew he had someone to turn to for help and guidance and this enabled him to build on his independence, express his feelings and feel cared for and loved within his safe, secure and warm family life.

Adam

Adam was 10 years old with two brothers: one younger, Martin aged 2; and one older, Paul aged 12. He lived in a large detached house in a busy Lancashire village with his brothers and parents. Adam's parents were both in their forties. His father owned his own business and typically left home after an early breakfast and arrived back in the evening at around 7 o'clock. During weekdays, Adam attended the local primary school, just a couple of minutes walk from his home. His mum was always at home to greet him on return from school. In the evenings and at weekends Adam was keen to play and watch sports, especially football. He also enjoyed playing computer games and pottering around at home, and playing with his pets: a goldfish and hamster.

Adam seemed to feel happy had content with his family life. When describing his family he said he felt:

Happiness, and laughter and sometimes, sometimes a bit of naughti-
ness . . . but playing games, going out to places with mum and dad . .
like 'Whirl'. Places like, sometimes like we go down to West Bay,
about three times a year to play in the sand dunes . . . I like it when
we go out to places, and like Wales and . . things like that.

Family outings were obviously a great source of pleasure to Adam. This was
a time when the whole family could enjoy themselves together. Otherwise,
each family member tended to disperse into different rooms in the house to
pursue their own interests. The size of the house was large enough for Adam
to feel lonely and isolated at times. Nevertheless, in his home he felt:

Nice and warm and it's quite big, so it's hard . . . so it takes quite a
long time to learn the actual way round the house.

Home was certainly a place he could bring friends to:

Adam: I like my bedroom, yeah, because it's quite a big room so . .
you can do quite a couple of things in there with my friends and they
can play.
Interviewer: What kind of things do you do?
Adam: Well mostly I'll play on my computer, but like if my friends
come we set up a game and play that. We tried Subuteo but [we]
broke the pieces as well, because we flicked it and one of the bits
broke.

Adam's parents set rules about where the children could play, and which areas
of the home were reserved for adults:

I like going to sit in mum and dad's sitting room because it's nice and
quiet in there and you never get disturbed. They don't really like us
going in.

Playing was not confined to the bedroom. Paul and Adam shared a sitting
room containing a snooker table and TV. Downstairs, the family room was
another location for the children to play in, as was the large back garden.

Despite the talk about playing, Adam seemed to have a sense of himself
as growing up and growing out of childhood games. Increasingly, he wanted
to take responsibility for making his own choices in what he did, where he
went and who he spent time with. Nevertheless he had to adhere to his
parents' ground rules about his behaviour and activities. He felt he had 'got
too old' for the local community centre club and had finished swimming lessons because he had 'learned how to swim, so I stopped that'. He occasionally
went to cricket or football training at the school, but this was a rare event.
While his everyday life was centred around his home and family, Adam was
allowed some independence in making everyday life decisions:

Interviewer: What kinds of things do you get to choose?
Adam: Well, if like my mum wants to get peace and quiet, I'll just say, 'I'm just playing out like for two hours,' and she'll say 'Yeah, you can go out.' And like I can choose if I want to play at my friend's, at my best friend's house, or play outside.

Concerning clothes and food, Adam was again allowed some choice:

I choose to wear tracksuit bottoms and sometimes, sometimes I get to choose what I want to eat. Sometimes she does me something. I like spaghetti and pizzas and pancakes which my mum sometimes makes me, if she feels up to it. But not very often.

Such freedoms were dependent on parental discretion which could be withdrawn for disciplinary reasons. Adam knew what the family rules were and that punishments he might expect for misbehaviour. Indeed, he felt that he was punished more often than his friends and for relatively minor misdemeanours:

Interviewer: What sort of things do you get told off for?
Adam: Whenever I'm late home playing out, and not like keeping the house tidy. They would probably ground me for the rest of the week.
Interviewer: Who tells you off the most?
Adam: Me dad. He'd be the one that would ground me . . [my friends] don't get told off as much as me.

Adam's perceptions of his parents were linked almost entirely to his own life, as if they had a limited existence outside of his own. He found it difficult to describe his parents in any detail. His father was seen as someone who decorated the house and played sporting activities with him. His mother shopped, cooked and cleaned but rarely played with the children:

Interviewer: How about you and your mum?
Adam: Sometimes I go out to the shops with her. In Rolston. Sometimes go out for a drive in the car. Drive round Earsley really, round the village.

In terms of household power structures, Adam saw his dad as the parent in overall control of family affairs:

If like mum and dad have an argument or something, my dad's always saying like you should all listen to him and everything. He always says that he's in charge of the house.

In many respects, the household was organized around the work and leisure schedule of Adam's father, including mealtimes, control of the TV remote and decisions about bedtime for the children. However, the main impression was one of a rather remote father. Indeed, one domain in which Adam's father was very much an outsider involved management of the emotional atmosphere in the family. Whenever Adam felt upset with friends or with school it was his brother and ultimately his mum to whom he turned for comfort and advice,

> I keep it all inside and then it all like works up so I end up telling my brother and then he tells my mum what's wrong. Not dad. Never dad.

Communication with his father revolved around sporting activities; unfortunately Adam felt he was a poor sportsman and found it difficult to live up to his father's expectations in this respect and, perhaps as a consequence, seemed to lack a little self-confidence. Adam constantly compared his relationship with his father to his brother Paul's relationship with his father, usually to his own self-deprecation:

> [I'm] not really a sportish person . . I just like to potter around . . My dad likes to play football and is really into loads of sports and . . billiards. My Dad's best. Best out of Paul and me, it's my brother, I'm no good at it.

On the other hand, when Adam had done well at school, both parents were involved in praising and rewarding his achievement:

> I think I did well in a . . on sports' day, because the team which I was in won. So my mum and dad were pleased with me for that.

The family system of rewards were well known to Adam and his brothers:

> They like let me play out for a bit longer, like an hour longer and sometimes they give me a bit of money for it, and like they just . . just like say 'well done' and things like that.

During Judith's time with Adam, he spent a lot of time considering his relationships with his two brothers. He was particularly eager to talk about Paul and the animosity that he felt existed between them:

> *Interviewer*: What about Paul? Is he a nice big brother?
> *Adam*: Not nice to me. He's always having fights with . . me . . he likes to ride around on his bike, round Earsley, going bike riding with dad.

> *Interviewer*: What gets your brother annoyed?
> *Adam*: If I do something which he wants to do. If I do . . something which he doesn't want to do and if he wants to do something I, if

he doesn't want to do something and I do it, we start fighting or something.
Interviewer: Do you mean fisticuffs or shouting at each other?
Adam: Both of them really.

Yet there were benefits to having a big brother in terms of being involved in more mature activities (football, cycling) and in having a person around to whom he could turn when he was upset.

Martin, Adam's younger brother was spoken of with more affection. Adam was keen to play with Martin on a level in which they both could have fun. Although, when games didn't work out Martin's way, things could get rough. Talking of his relationship with Martin, Adam said:

Sometimes I like him, other times I don't, but he likes playing around and we play hide-and-seek and tig in the back garden . . I have to do what he chooses. If I don't do what he wants, he'll start pulling my hair and pinching me.

Although the main discussion with Adam focused very much on his immediate family. Adam did expand his family tree to include his grandparents (both sets), aunties, uncles and cousins. The extended family lived in close proximity to Earsley village.

Adam would sometimes cycle to visit his grandparents and occasionally sleep over, a treat he particularly enjoyed. He felt he could talk openly with his grandparents and they would play and laugh together. In addition, his mother's parents have taken him on holiday in the past, and a trip to Legoland in Denmark was planned as a treat for his next birthday and Christmas present combined. There were also enjoyable outings with one of his three uncles, when uncle Peter would take Adam, Paul and cousin Ellen to the swimming baths. Other than this, Adam had little contact with his aunties, uncles and five younger cousins.

Finally, Adam thought about what kind of family he would like to have when he grew up:

Interviewer: When you grow up and maybe have a family, what would you want that family to be like?
Adam: A fun family which is always going out to places and doing good stuff, like, and if I have children let them choose on what they want to do.

This idealistic notion of family life was clearly rooted in the most enjoyable aspects of his own life and reflected the expectations he felt his parents had of his behaviour as well as his increasing sense of independence and choice.

'Traditional' Family Life: Children's Perspectives

There were a number of similarities between the concerns, ideas and experiences of the two children that Judith talked to despite the fact that Jonathan was an only child, while Adam had two brothers. The security, warmth, predictability and support of family life came across very clearly in both cases. Their efforts to build relationships with family members (and friends) and to interpret and develop their relationships within the family context were obviously critical aspects of everyday family life. The boys were constantly in the process of negotiating the meaning of family life with their family, whether this was through sibling rivalry and friendship in Adam's case, or through the sharing of joint interests in Jonathan's case.

The entanglement of family emotions within the home was an important issue for the boys. As Woollett (1986) has intimated, emotional exchanges extend between all family members; children and their parents, as well as between siblings. This was evident in the children's experience of discipline within the home as well as their efforts to deal with sibling rivalry and conflict. Such emotionally charged exchanges did not appear to affect the boys' conceptions of their homes as secure and happy, but were simply encountered as part-and-parcel of intimate family life.

Perhaps one of the key issues that emerged for Judith, as an active listener in the process of the sessions, was the way in which each of the boys conceived of their home. Research into the meaning of home has repeatedly revealed the home to be much more than the bricks and mortar with which it is built (Hayward, 1977; Lawrence, 1991). Home has been identified as a place of happiness and belonging, responsibility and self-expression, privacy and security (Hayward, 1977; Sixsmith, 1986; Depres, 1991). The central role of the home as a physical location for family-based activities as well as a centre for the sharing of family lives has been well documented (Depres, 1991; Sixsmith and Sixsmith, 1990, 1991). These empirical studies of the meaning of home have been conducted with adult samples. The boys in the present study both gave a sense of their home as a safe haven from the outside world, a place of sharing and belonging, privacy and happiness, and the main location for their everyday activities. Family rituals and rules concerning conduct, special occasions and chores were all well understood by the boys and contributed to a sense of belonging within the family and the home.

Within the context of home and family life both boys saw their mother's role as markedly different to their father's role. Mum was seen as a key figure in structuring family routines. The importance of the mother figure has been stressed in family research (Winnicott, 1964), yet both boys had little knowledge of their mum's everyday life. Indeed, mums were very much taken for granted as they played an almost background role in supporting the family with housework, cooking and through emotional turmoil. In contrast, the boys' fathers seemed to figure largely as parents involved in play and leisure-time activities, despite their work commitments which kept them out of the home for long periods. Neither boy felt that they could approach their father with emotional problems. Both boys wanted to live up to their father's expectations and met with varying degrees of success in this respect.

The fathers appeared to act as role models for the boys. Neither father was involved in housework, just as neither of the boys felt that it was their role to perform work tasks within the family home. This brings to mind Leach's (1994) argument that modern children in western society are rarely expected to work within the family and, indeed, that childhood is mainly conceptualized in terms of play and education. This is particularly so in the relationship between boys and housework. The division of labour within traditional family life continues to impose the responsibility for housework predominantly on female family members (Demo and Acock, 1993) and so supports the continuation of gendered family roles. The boys in the present study certainly felt that housework was the preserve of their mothers. By failing to witness (and be part of) a more egalitarian division of housework in their own families, the boys may have begun to structure their thoughts and expectations for their own future families (Goldscheider and Waite, 1991) along gendered family role structures.

For both of the boys, home was also a place in which they were learning to become increasingly independent. Jonathan and Adam valued their time outside of the home when visiting friends or relatives. Both had constructed a lifestyle which had interwoven their family, social and educational life. Indeed, social lives outside of the home were structured by the constraints of family life in that parents had the ultimate say about where the children were allowed to go and at what time they were due to return. The family, the child and their life outside of the home were all, as Ingleby (1986) suggests, interconnected and interrelated.

Despite the similarities identified above, there were also differences in the ways in which each household operated (from the children's perspective). There were differences in the ways in which the parents made themselves available to the children. Adam spent much less time with his father than did Jonathan, whose main interests and hobbies often embraced his father as a partner. Adam's father was perceived as the person in control of the household, a somewhat remote figure who played sports and imposed family discipline. Jonathan's relationship with his father was warm and intimate, based more on shared activities than rules and regulations. While Adam's time at home revolved mainly around playing (and fighting) with his brothers or watching TV, Jonathan spent more time with his father and mother. He enjoyed chatting to his mother in the kitchen after school (instead of doing homework!) and felt confident that she would help him through any personal difficulties.

Everyday life in the traditional family was evidently viewed from these two children's perspectives as happy, intimate, emotional and complex. It was a space where relationships with family members and friends were worked out, interests and activities were pursued and privacy and belonging were secured. For these children, at least, the traditional family was a nice place to be.

Thinking Points

- Write an account of the most 'traditional family' with which you have personal experience. Describe issues relating to the developing gender identities of children in the family. To what extent do these reflect contemporary images of male and female parents? Why is this question important?

- What are the valuable dimensions of conflict and tension in family life? How do the emotional ups and downs of private family life influence a child's public social life? Try to augment your thinking with observations from your own experience of emotionally charged events in family life.

- Follow an account of a family experiencing conflict in current newspapers. What are the differences between acceptable conflict within family life and unacceptable conflict? Discuss your views with someone else and consider the origins and significance of any differences of perception and interpretation.

- Think about the 'traditional family' twenty years hence. What features of 'traditional family' life would you hope remain intact? Having reflected on what the children in this chapter have had to say, do you think there should be more or less emphasis on 'traditional family' types? What factors might influence the endurance of the 'traditional family'?

Chapter 3

Families with Parents Who have Multiple Commitments

Carolyn Kagan and Suzan Lewis

Introduction

This chapter draws on the accounts of children whose parents have multiple commitments in terms of combining work with caring for both disabled and non-disabled children, and/or elderly relatives. We know it is stressful combining work with family life (Lewis and Cooper, 1988); we are just beginning to learn about how families manage to combine work with additional caring, such as caring for a sick or disabled relative; caring for elders; or caring for disabled or chronically sick children (Baldwin, 1985; Baldwin and Glendinning, 1983; Beresford, 1995; Kagan and Lewis, 1995; Parker, 1990), and how people negotiate responsibilities within families (Finch and Mason, 1993). We know little about what it is like for children within these families (Baldwin and Carlisle, 1994), although other studies on caring have alluded to the possibility that they may experience family life very differently from their parents (Macaskill, 1985; Zirinsky, 1994).

Whilst there is interest and concern for parents of learning disabled children and their experiences of caring, brothers and sisters are rarely considered. What this suggests, we think, is that their experiences are thought to be irrelevant to the ways in which families manage. Indeed, many parents say explicitly that they do not want to place extra burdens on their sons and daughters as a result of their having multiple commitments, although they do worry that they are unable to give all their children sufficient time (Beresford, 1995). Children within these families are immediately placed at the receiving end of what Franklin (1986) describes as arbitrary parental authority, in terms of decisions they (the parents) have made along with their underlying assumptions. This authority in turn leads to both family practices and the provision of supports to families that take no account of the perspectives or experiences of the children. Franklin (1986) describes the way in which this type of arbitrary parental authority, amongst other things, denies children fundamental rights to a say in the progress of their own lives. The least we can do to reassert their rights is to listen to what the children say.

We bring to the chapter a number of things. We both have children and partners who have always worked full-time. Quite a lot of our work over the last ten years has been with families who support and care for learning disabled children, of whatever age. Only occasionally have we met brothers and sisters. This chapter provides an opportunity for a few of these children to have their views listened to and taken seriously.

Who is Talking?

Carolyn Kagan took responsibility for interviewing the children whose accounts are central to this chapter. Seven boys were asked about their experiences of life within families that have multiple commitments for work and caring. Of course, the stories heard depend on who is asked. With this in mind, Carolyn specifically sought children from families that she knew, each with different kinds of multiple commitments. Families were chosen for a number of reasons. Firstly, at least one family, where parents had multiple commitments to work, children and, additionally to a disabled child or elderly relative, was known through work. Secondly, families were believed to be two parent families. Thirdly, she had not met the children before in any other context. Fourthly, the families seemed to reflect different parental assumptions about the rights of children. In this respect, one large family, with four boys, (known here as the Greens), operated on democratic principles, where the children were enabled to make active decisions about family life. In another family with one boy (known here as the Smiths), the parents believed that the needs of children were best understood in terms of understanding the needs of the family. There were two boys from a family in which the parents worried about their fragmented family lifestyle and the effect it might have on the children (known here as the Bells). They felt they had an overriding responsibility to ensure their children's happiness. In each case, a parent was contacted first, who then asked their sons if they would be willing to talk about their experiences of family life for this book.

We feel that it would be too much of a breach of trust given by the boys to compromise their anonymity. The problem is that parents and other family members might recognize the children if too much personal and family detail is given. This means that we will not indicate to which family which boy belongs. Instead, we will relate their experiences in a more general way, in the full knowledge that something will be lacking in not being able to relate these experiences either to what their brothers may have said, or to their specific family circumstances. (In the Smith family, though, there is only one boy, and his family circumstances mean that it has been impossible to conceal his identity all of the time. This was discussed with him and he was shown the extracts we wished to use for this discussion and he has given his permission for them to be included.) Where there is agreement between the boys within a family, this is indicated, but we will not reveal what any one particular boy has said.

Where there is disagreement within a family, particular statements are not linked with particular boys.

The stories are all told by white boys. This helps preserve anonymity, as it would have been easier to identify particular individuals, with such a small number of participants, if girls or black children had been involved. We are aware that this is, perhaps, an unsatisfactory compromise to an ethical dilemma, and that the accounts will necessarily be gendered and Anglocentric. It is also an arbitrary compromise as the participants could equally have been all girls, or black. The boys (by age, not by family) are: Mark 17; James 15; Alex 14; Daniel 12; Iain 12; Ben 10; Sam 10.

The Families

The Greens live in a village and have four boys aged between 10 and 17. The youngest boy has Downs Syndrome and was adopted at 6 months; he gave his own account of family life.[1] In this family, both parents work in the caring and education professions.

The Smiths live in a northern town. Their children are a 10-year-old boy with a 6-year-old sister who is lively and demanding even though she uses a wheelchair, has no speech and requires assistance with most of the tasks of daily living. She often has to go into hospital for several days at a time. Father is a window fitter and mother works at weekends in an elderly persons' home and on Friday nights as a barmaid.

The Bells live in a suburb of a northern city. The family consists of two boys, aged 12 and 14 years old, living with mother and father and great aunt, who has lived with them from January–June for the last four years. Mother used to work as a youth worker but is now a fulltime student. Father has worked abroad for the last three years as an executive in a multinational company, returning for a week about every three months.

How Did the Boys Tell Their Stories?

At their request, Carolyn talked to each boy separately in their own homes. At least one parent was present in the house, but the discussion was in private. Four conversations were tape-recorded and notes taken from the rest. The illustrations of the boys stories have been lifted directly from tapes or notes. The accuracy of quotes from notes was checked with the boys concerned. At

---

[1] Whilst I have included the picture the youngest Green boy drew with me of who was in his family, I have included little else of our conversation about family life. I spent about an hour talking with him, and this was not long enough to get good information about what he thought about his family. He has some difficulty communicating complex ideas through speech, and I would have had to use a number of different symbolic techniques, mostly through play and from a position of our knowing each other better, in order to do him justice in writing about how he experiences family life. Both he and I enjoyed our hour together and I am pleased to be able to include some of the material he gave me. (Carolyn Kagan)

the end of each conversation, the boys were left with a blank piece of paper and asked to let us have a picture of what *family* meant to them. The youngest of the Greens drew a picture of his family during our conversation. Indeed, this was the best way to discuss family life with him and to help him concentrate. The Bell and Smith boys each constructed a family tree as part of our conversations, whereas the Green boys did not: Carolyn constructed an impressionistic family tree based on the conversations with each of the children. Similarly, the Bell and Smith boys were asked specifically about relationships within their families and how these might be mapped onto the family trees.

Listening to the tapes revealed several emergent themes, not specifically linked to the caring responsibilities within the family as anticipated, but rather to features of family life that gave the boys an anchor in life, where 'family' was a community to which each boy belonged. The following discussion will consider how the boys define the boundaries of their family communities and then go on to consider the rules, rituals and role responsibilities they identify within their families. In doing this, we are attempting to interpret their 'insider' views for 'outsiders' like ourselves and you, the reader.

Children's Reflections

Family Boundaries

There was wide agreement amongst all boys as to what constituted their family. All of them started off by defining family in terms of household: family is those that live here. This meant that some of the people ordinarily considered as part of the wider kinship structure were not included in the boys' conceptions of their family.

The Bell boys were particularly interesting in this respect. Both boys (separately) initially excluded their father from their descriptions of their family. As one of them put it:

> *Child*: There's me . . [brother], and me Mum . . er . . Aunt Polly is here sometimes.
> *Interviewer*: Anyone else? they don't have to be in the house always.
> *Child*: Oh! I suppose there's me dad. [*laughs*] I guess you'd better include him. . . . me Uncle Jack's got three children, they're cousins. We see them a bit, Janet, Elaine, William and Susie . . do they count?
> *Interviewer*: Could do, anyone else?
> *Child*: What, cousins, do you mean?
> *Interviewer*: [*shrugs*]
> *Child*: No. More uncles and that . . but that's not really me family.

Later on, when talking about who does what with whom in the family, both boys mentioned their dad without hesitation. Figure 3.1 shows the boys' perceptions of the composition of the Bell family.

Figure 3.1 Boys' representation of the Bell family

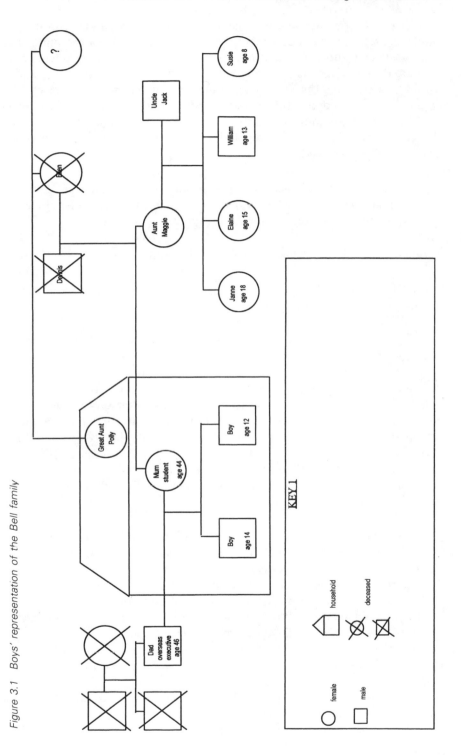

All of the boys in the Green family, too, drew a boundary around the family that solely contained members of the household. After prompting, they, too, mentioned aunts and cousins. One of the boys also included grand-parents. He suggested that cousins would be included in the family, and so would their children, but that a line would be drawn at second cousins. Two of the boys pointed out that living far away and not seeing them much made it difficult to think of cousins as family. When talking about other aspects of family life, however, the wider family group were included without hesitation. One boy said:

> I go to my aunt's at Easter. Have done for ages. . . . there's an Easter egg hunt . . cream eggs all over the house and I have to find them. Usually this takes sort of all day. It's good.

Another mentioned at a different point in the conversation:

> Well, yes, we all know . . my mother's sister . . that's my aunt . . has Downs Syndrome, so I suppose there's nothing unusual in it.

Figure 3.2 shows the family composition according to the three eldest boys of the Green family.

The youngest of the Greens was the most concrete of all the boys in describing his family. He went beyond those people who **live** in the household to describe all those who were **in the house that day** as members of his family. This included the interviewer (Carolyn) and her two daughters, who had just had lunch with the family, as well as the family cat (see Figure 3.3).

The Smith boy, however, went beyond the immediate household to include his grandmother (but not the aunt who lives with her) in his description of his family. He described it thus:

> *Child*: Well . . . there's me gran. She's me mam's mam. I go to her if I have to. Then there's me da', me mam and Anna [sister]. But you'll know about Anna. She doesn't talk and that.
> *Interviewer*: Anyone else? Cousins and that?
> *Child*: Shelly and Louise. They're cousins. I think I might have some too on his [father] side but they don't talk to us . . since Anna . . I think . . well, it's more me da' cut them off, he told me.

Figure 3.4 illustrates the boys' perceptions of the composition of the Smith family.

Knowing who is in the family does not give us much sense of what the different family members mean to the boys. Carolyn asked them all to describe who does what and with whom in the family. Within these parts of the

Figure 3.2 The Green family (derived from conversations with the boys)

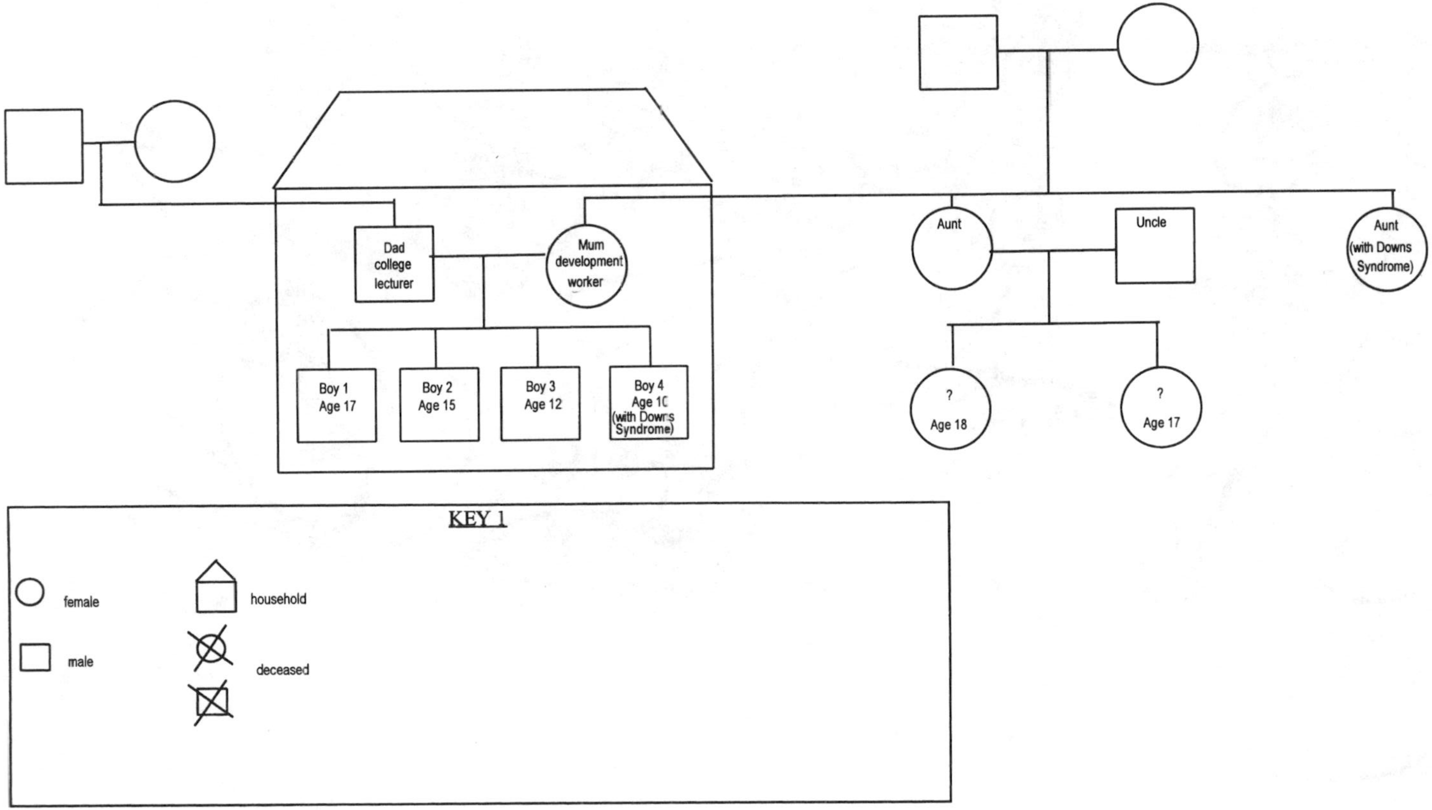

Aunt (with Downs Syndrome)

Uncle

? Age 17

Aunt

? Age 18

Mum development worker

Dad college lecturer

Boy 1 Age 17

Boy 2 Age 15

Boy 3 Age 12

Boy 4 Age 10 (with Downs Syndrome)

KEY 1

female ○

male □

household

deceased

Figure 3.3 The Green family as drawn by the youngest boy

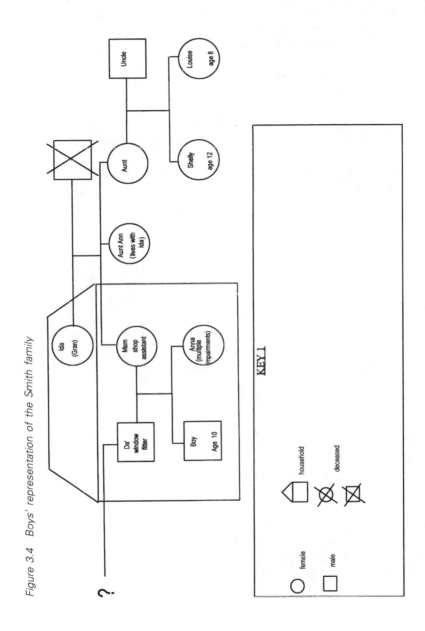

Figure 3.4 Boys' representation of the Smith family

conversations, the way in which each boy thinks the family works as a system of relationships was revealed.

The Green boys all gave examples of activities and illustrations of the likes and dislikes between members of the family. Whilst the examples of positive and negative family relationships were different, they all led to the same picture of alliances and exclusions within the immediate family. For example, in describing how one brother conforms less than the others, three of the boys made the point with reference to a different example. One boy told the following story:

[My brother] will get annoyed when [my other brother and I] are playing football or cricket in the garden. I'm very competitive .. we're always playing for points. Sometimes we'll let him play with us .. we'll give him a couple of lives. Sometimes he doesn't mind. Sometimes he'll go off complaining about how it's not fair and he's not getting a fair deal. It makes it very difficult to include him and sometimes we just don't bother any more.

One of his brothers said:

I hate the way I'm treated. The others get everything and I get nothing. We all have to buy things for our lunches at school but [two of my brothers] get the lunch money and their pocket money in the summer .. I don't get my lunch money .. I just get the same [money as my younger brother] even though I'm two years older. .... When I say 'it's not fair' to Mum and Dad, they take no notice.

A third brother commented that:

[My brother] is always going into my room and taking things. I think he does it because he feels left out or something .. just trying to get attention. Whenever [my other brother] and I are watching television, he will want something different and then there's a row. Now he's got his own television in his room it's a bit better.

The impressionistic picture of family relationships Carolyn gained from the Green boys' accounts is shown in Figure 3.5.

The family is united over their liking for and their efforts to get on with the youngest boy (who has Downs Syndrome). One of the boys said, as part of a discussion about who gets on with whom:

We all get on with [our youngest brother] and he gets on with everyone. I don't think he really has favourites. You couldn't not really. He likes everyone .. very likeable. We let him join in whatever we're doing, but he usually gets fed up after a bit and goes off.

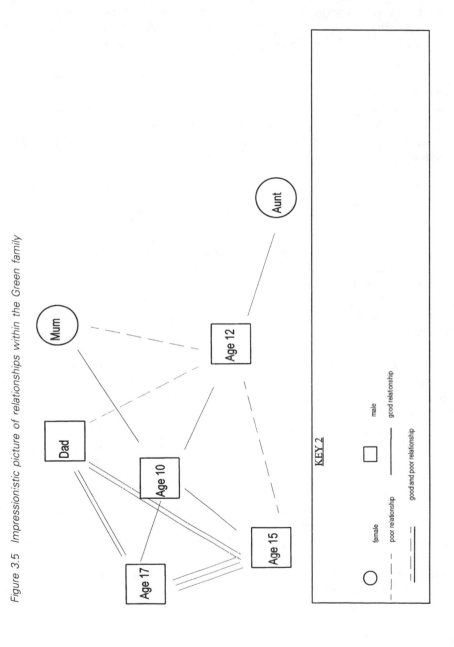

Figure 3.5 Impressionistic picture of relationships within the Green family

The three older boys were interested in playing football and cricket (and golf for the two eldest). They belonged to sports clubs and played in the garden, sometimes with their father. A large proportion of time was spent talking about sport, and no mention was made of their mother as a participant in these activities. None of the boys mentioned any time spent specifically with their mother which is why, in Figure 3.5, Carolyn has placed her on her own within the family.

When the Smith boy described his family, he restricted his account to his immediate family (Anna, mother, father and gran), but described subsystems of relationships within it. Figure 3.6 shows the picture of the Smith family relationships that he and Carolyn drew in conversation together.

Initially, the way he spoke was as if he were an only child, excluding his disabled sister:

> I'm on my own. It's lonely sometimes. There's no-one here for me. My friends are good, and I see them a lot . . I [also] spend a lot of time in my room.

He talked of how he gets on with his gran better than with his parents:

> Me gran, and me . . we're on our own . . when she's [Anna] in hospital I go to me gran's or she comes here. I can talk to her. She's me mate at home. The others [mother and father] don't bother with me. It's all about her [Anna].

He saw himself and his gran as a pair, quite separate from the other three members of the family. At one point in the conversation, talking about relationships within the family, he said:

> This has been really good. I've never really thought about it before. I see now why I think it's only me gran what cares [about me]. The others, they care about Anna. I suppose they have to, she's sick so much and can't do nothing herself . . it's not really that they don't care, I suppose, more that there's no time. She's in hospital a lot, they've got to be there . . . I think . . I hate her. No, I think I *did* hate her, for making them [mother and father] not bother [with me]. Talking here, now, I think that's not right. They haven't got time. It ain't her fault.

He does not like Anna, although he says that he has never had to think about it before, and certainly, perhaps more crucially, has not been asked about it before:

> *Child:* Anna? No, I don't play with Anna. What's the point? All me life it's Anna this and Anna that . . never [me] . . [*looking straight at Carolyn, and away from the paper on which he's been drawing his family*] . .

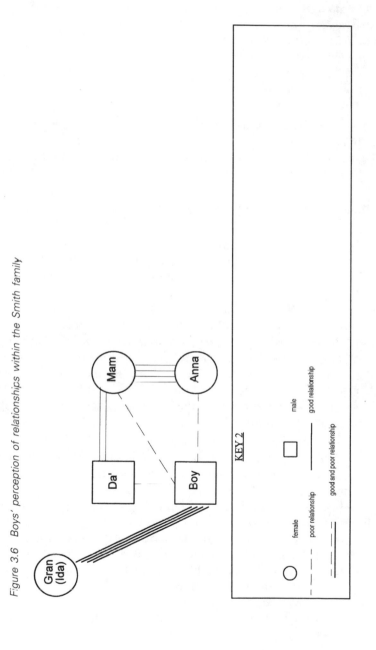

Figure 3.6 Boys' perception of relationships within the Smith family

Sometimes I'd like to push her right out her chair . . I'm not meant to
say that, but it's true . . . Have you seen her eat? [*doesn't wait for reply*]
She dribbles. Yuk! I've had friends here . . [*looks out of window and
stops talking*].
Interviewer: And?
Child: . . . And I've not wanted them back because of the way she is.
Interviewer: Have they come back?
Child: Yes. yes they have. [*looks at me*] . . So they can't have minded
can they? I've not thought that before. I'll tell me gran!

After having this conversation, he was keen to add something to the picture
of family relationships.

Figure 3.7 shows that he added a tentative link between himself and his
sister, because, as he put it:

I think I might be able to like her better now.

It is clear from this extract, and certainly to Carolyn from having had the
conversation with him, that he gained some insight into his own feelings and
experiences, as well as into his relationships with his sister, from the conversation. No-one had asked him about it before, and although it was not easy
for him to talk about it, he was pleased he had done so.

The Bells both described their family in similar terms when asked who
was in it. However, when they were asked about who did what with whom,
two very different pictures of family relationships emerged. One of the boys
included Aunt Polly, who lives with them for six months of the year as a
member of the close knit family relationships. He liked her and enjoyed helping her at the shops and does not mind reading to her, even if it is the same
things she wants to read to her over and over again. As he said:

Child: Aunt Polly is definitely one of us. I'd put her close to mum and
to me. I help her a lot. Quite like it really, it's not hard. A bit of a drag
sometimes but overall. OK. I help her at the shops. It's quite a laugh
really because she gets in a bit of a muddle. They're [the shopkeepers]
all right round here. Try to help out and that . . Sometimes I read her
mag for her. It's better than the telly blaring out some rubbish. She
reads . . what is it now? . . 'People's Friend', that's it. There's not much
that's fit . . but it's OK. Gets a bit boring when it's the same bits she
wants read. I reckon it's OK really.
Interviewer: What do your friends think of it?
Child: Don't know. Never really said. I don't think they'd bother.
There's lots round here got someone living [with them]. Some lots
worse than Aunt Polly. [My brother] doesn't bother much. I think
mum's pleased I help . . there's quite a . . you know . . [flurry of

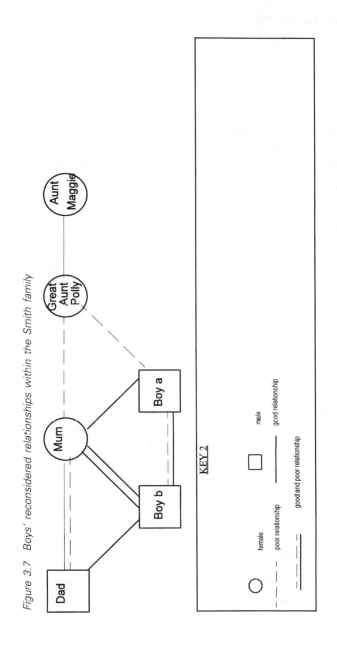

Figure 3.7 Boys' reconsidered relationships within the Smith family

KEY 2

○ female   ☐ male

- - - poor relationship   ——— good relationship

——— good and poor relationship

activity] when she's due to come . . mum gets all worked up . . I just help a bit.

His brother, on the other hand, did not consider Aunt Polly to be central to the family. If anything, he resented her coming:

> *Interviewer*: What about Aunt Polly?
> *Child*: She's out on her own . . caught between us and Aunt Maggie, I suppose. She's certainly not close in this family. I'd put myself a long way apart from her. It's a drag when she's here. I can't stand it. He [brother] doesn't seem to mind as much. But me . . I don't like mum getting all uptight. I think I look out for her more. Then she yells at dad when he's home. It doesn't happen when she's [Aunty Polly] not here. I don't see why she can't be in a home or whatever. We haven't got the room. I wouldn't even put her in there with [my brother] and certainly not with me mum.

Whilst there is some agreement between the two of them as to their relative relationship with Aunt Polly, their pictures of overall family relationships differ from each other's. Most of the boys' time within the family was spent with each other: they did relatively little with either parent. As one of them put it:

> *Child*: We go round with [each other] I guess, but it's mostly with mates. Perhaps we'll listen to tapes or watch TV. Mum sometimes watches TV, but mostly she works . . the back room is more or less hers. When dad's home, mum and him do a lot of stuff . . we don't really bother.
> *Interviewer*: Has it always been like that?
> *Child*: Well, I guess when we were little . . dad was home . . football, swimming, things like that. Mum used to go to the park . . that's it really.

His brother confirmed this account:

> We don't do much really. Eat, when dad's home. Hang around. I go out a lot . . rather be at me mate's. Sometimes [my brother] comes. Did play football and that, but I'm not really interested so much . . . Mum? She's just there really.

We can see from these descriptions of family relationships that different children within the same family have different experiences and perceptions of how members of the family relate together. However, we can also see that there is common ground between the different members of the same family. Understandings of family relationships are jointly constructed by the members of the family. The children, when giving their accounts of the family in single conversational interviews like these, partly reproduce the constructed accounts of relationships within the family. The individual differences in perceptions of family life became more apparent when we talked together about those family rules, rituals and role responsibilities that guided each boy's behaviour.

Rules and Rituals

All of the boys reported some family 'rules' which were sometimes formally agreed within the family, and informal rules with which all members of the family tacitly agreed:

> *1st child*: I think it's agreed we don't go into each other's rooms and take things out, although [one of my brothers] sometimes breaks this rule.
> *2nd child*: We all do our jobs, we have a kind of rota. You know, tidying our room, drying up and that.
> *Interviewer*: What would happen if you didn't?
> *2nd child*: Dunno — we all just do them. Sometimes mum has to nag us a bit.
> *3rd child*: When dad's home we have tea together round the table. When he's not there, we just have it where we want.
> *4th child*: As long as I tell them where I'm going, I can be out all day.
>
> *1st child*: We always .. don't know why .. we always get mum's breakfast ready when Aunt Polly's here. She doesn't make us, it just happens like that, but we both know we have to do it. I suppose we both know she's got a lot to do for Aunt Polly before she goes out.
> *2nd child*: Rules? Mustn't be rotten to Anna. That's the rule here.

The youngest Green boy did not talk about anything that could be called a family rule. Carolyn spent quite a bit of time with each boy talking about the ways in which discipline was upheld in their families, and they talked about this in ways which described, at times, complex family rituals. The Smith boy described what happens to him when he is getting told off:

> It's always the same. Me mam, she yells at me. I don't really take much notice. She then yells at me da' and he don't take much notice. She wants him to tell me, but he won't. So she yells some more. I might do it or I might not. In the end I'll probably get a belt or not watch telly. There's nowt they can do really .. With me gran it's different. She can make me feel bad .. and good. She just talks to me, usually about how hard it is for mam and da'. Then I feel bad.

The three eldest Green boys all agreed that their mother and father told them off equally. They also agreed how punishments were meted out. As one of them put it:

Mum thinks about it more and finds something that will really affect us. Dad gets into a rage .. says whatever comes into his head, and kind of roars, but that's it .. doesn't really bother us. It's much worse when it's Mum.

The Bell boys disagreed about what happened in their family. Whilst they agreed that it was their mother that told them off most of the time, they disagreed about what happened when their father came home, and how it was that discipline was maintained in their family. One of them said:

It's always mum that does it. She's very calm and shows us how disappointed she is in us. She makes us feel terrible, really small. It's just the same when dad is home, though then she does go a bit spare too .. shouts and that, but mostly at him not us.

The other put it like this:

Mum's cross all the time. She's always shouting and in a [bad] temper. Sometimes she just goes crazy. After a while we just sort of get used to it. I don't think it's us she's cross at. More just everything she has to do. I think she's tired, too. When dad's home, he joins in. You know, shouting and that — mostly at us, yes, that's it. It's worse in the summer, because Aunt Polly gets right up his . . .

The Bells are picking up some of the stresses their parents experience in living their complex lives. However, they cope with this by postulating some of the causes of their parents' irritation and almost taking on responsibility for their well-being. All of the boys, in one way or another, talked about the responsibilities they felt they had as members of their families, and linked to this what the importance of family was to them.

Role Responsibilities

Mark, Alex and Sam were all the oldest child in their families. This brought with it certain privileges, but linked responsibilities. One of them captured the advantages of being the first to do things when he said:

I've been the first to do things — like go to a '12' film. I haven't had particular restrictions put on me being first . . . For the past few years I've had to look after [brother] .. like if mum and dad go out. But if I wanted to go out when they wanted me to look after [brother] I'd be allowed to and they'd make other arrangements. On the whole, I do have more responsibility for people and things .. but it's both good and bad.

One of them, however, thought that being the oldest gave him much more, unwelcome, responsibility:

> *Child*: Everything is my fault. I'm expected to stop him [brother] getting into bother. How can I? It's always been me that is told 'do this, do that', never him. I have to get straight home from school so [my brother] doesn't have to come home to the house alone. But I have to.
>
> *Interviewer*: Do you like doing this?
>
> *Child*: Not particularly. But no-one asks me. I'm just expected not to mind. It's like I'm another parent or something.

The final 'first child' also felt he was expected to be mature, but rather liked this:

> *Child*: They [parents] have always made out I know what to do and can do it. That's OK. Makes you grow right up. I like that.
>
> *Interviewer*: What is it you like about it?
>
> *Child*: No-one bothers you. Just do what you like. No-one can call *me* me mammy's boy!

None of the boys elsewhere in the family talked about his particular responsibilities, with the exception of the Green boys in relation to their disabled brother. Each Green boy considered it part of his family responsibility to look out for this brother and to help out if he was agitated or confused about things. This was reflected in different comments the boys made. For example, one of them said:

> Sometimes I have to deal with [my youngest brother] .. like if he's being a pain on the bus .. me or [one of my other brothers] might have to go with him and then get our own bus to school. It's OK .. as long as I'm not late for school.

However, the youngest boys in the families talked about how they hated the way others treated them and assumed they were too babyish to do things. One of them said:

> It's all right [for my older brother], he can do anything he likes. Me, no-one ever thinks I can do anything. I'm not even allowed down the field with a mate, but it's, 'Where are you going? When will you be back?' .. I don't know what they think will happen. And with him [brother] he thinks he can just tell me to do this and tell me off and that. Just like he was me dad or something.

In a similar vein, the other one said:

> It's not fair the way I'm treated. I get nothing. They treat me like I was
> a baby .. have done ever since I can remember. I suppose to them
> I was the baby, but not now. That's why I like going away [by myself].

It seems, then, that for these boys their position as eldest or youngest in the
family gave them more in common with each other, in terms of responsibility
or lack of it, than the particular family in which they lived.

Whatever their particular experiences of their own families, all of the boys
praised family life for the security it gave them. They compared themselves
favourably with other families they knew, and could anticipate their future
families in terms of similarities with, and differences from, their present families. Some were somewhat ambiguous in their praise, as in this summing up:

> I wouldn't have any other family .. Just wish I wasn't discriminated
> against so unfairly. I wouldn't wish for different family .. just wish
> they were all more decent to me.

Also ambiguous, but in a different way, was this comment:

> I thought I hated them [my family]. [I] wished I had another one. Now
> I think it's OK. Good even. When I think of me mates, they're no
> better off. We're all the same.

One of the Bell brothers talked of two different families, one with and one
without Aunt Polly.

> It's great, me brother and me mum and me dad .. when he's here.
> I think I'm lucky to have them. But I hate it when she [Aunt Polly]
> comes. It all changes. Then we are different from others, I mean, I
> don't think most of my friends are meant to go round helping old
> ladies. And I don't think they would.

His brother had a different view:

> My family is where I feel safe. Loved I suppose. It's a shame dad isn't
> with us. I wouldn't have my mum stay at home. Why should she?
> When Aunt Polly comes, then .. when .. sort of .. you know, it all
> seems right. What families are for. Caring for each other. What else are
> they for?

One of the other boys said he thought families were much of a muchness.
He commented that:

> All families are the same really aren't they? They're all OK. Both the
> same and different. Each one .. ours too .. is unique, but otherwise

the same. You're friends with your family, that's the most important thing. And you're made to feel you're important, that you matter.

The oldest boy that Carolyn spoke to summed up the importance of families thus:

> [With families] there's always someone there to support you. Stand up for you like if you haven't done so well at football. They pick you up a bit . . . [Families] help you cope with things. You can't have everything you want in life. They help you see you're part of a group. They allow you to contribute something to other people, not just take from them.

Families with Multiple Commitments: Children's Perspectives

The boys whose reflections are given in this chapter had positive and negative experiences of family life. Their views both coincided with and differed from those of their brothers. Whilst they were happy to discuss their experiences of having working parents, none of them thought this particularly remarkable and took it in their stride. As their comments showed, at times some of the stresses experienced by parents rubbed off on the children and they expressed a degree of protectiveness towards their parents, particularly their mothers. The boys in the largest family (the Greens) considered other family dynamics to be more important than the fact of having a disabled brother, although their disabled brother was clearly important to them and gave them opportunities for loving, caring and making a contribution that they would not otherwise have had. They had a common understanding of how their brothers might experience the family life they shared, and, as insiders to the family, presented a particular face of family life to Carolyn, the outsider. Had just one of the boys been spoken to, only one version of this public face of the family would have been laid open. By speaking to them all, a view of how the same acts and activities within the family are experienced by different children was uncovered. This highlights the importance of recognizing and seeking individual children's accounts, and of not assuming there is only one 'true' account of family life. Whilst children within a family may learn the same family 'script' their accounts of playing their particular roles within the family will differ. This point will be returned to in the concluding chapter of this book.

The above point was illustrated further by the Bell boys. Theirs was a smaller family with less stability over time. The family scripts were less well developed and learnt, and consequently there was greater discrepancy in the boys' accounts of family life. Despite this, each boy gave different accounts of common experiences. The two boys had more in common with oldest and youngest boys from other families than they had with each other. They reacted differently to the additional caring responsibilities undertaken by the family for half of each year. One boy found this a positive opportunity, the other felt restricted. Again, this highlights the importance of not assuming commonality within families: different children experience in different ways the multiple family commitments in which they are embroiled. Had Carolyn only spoken to either one of these boys, a quite different impression of the effect of having Aunt Polly to live with them would have been gained.

One interesting point here is the revelation of the Bell boys as young carers of their elderly Aunt. Olsen (1996) has pointed out that very little is known about the experiences of children involved in caring responsibilities. We see in this chapter that the boys reacted very differently to their caring role. As such, we have begun to reveal both the pleasures and the drawbacks of children taking on a caring role. Further research in this vein will help to develop our existing awareness about the relationship between caring and childhood.

Talking to the son of the Smiths raised some completely different issues. Here was a boy who had no other siblings with whom he could relate, and chose, instead, to forge a sibling-type relationship with his grandmother. His experience of having working parents caring for a severely disabled sister was almost completely negative. Until our conversation, he reported that he had not been asked about how he felt about his sister, or family life before. He said that talking for the purposes of this research gave him a sense of being considered important and valued. He appeared to gain considerable insight into his relationship with both his parents and his sister. What this highlights is not only the neediness and loneliness of some children within families whose parents have multiple commitments, but the value of giving children the opportunity to talk about their caring responsibilities and family commitments. The Green and the Bell boys at least had brothers with whom they could discuss the joys and tribulations of everyday life. However, whilst larger families could offer some support and respite, all three of the older Green boys said that they would probably not have four children themselves — two would be better!

As pointed out earlier on, the conversations on which this chapter is based were all with white, English boys. Their accounts of family life and of the commitments that go with working parents and additional caring responsibilities will necessarily be gendered and Anglocentric. Their concerns, relationships with each other and with their different parents may well be culturally and gender specific. However, their accounts include positive experiences of caring (traditionally associated with girls and women), and reveal different kinds of relationships with mothers and fathers. From these seven conversations it would be impossible to speculate on common family experiences of boys as such, or boys' experiences as different from girls. Nevertheless, they do show how important it is not to make assumptions about the capacities of boys to fulfil caring responsibilities within families, or not.

The overriding conclusion is that there may be as many different accounts of living in families with multiple commitments as there are children. We cannot say the experience is unequivocally positive or negative. Nor is it remarkable. Finch and Mason (1993) found something similar in their qualitative study of family responsibilities:

> These experiences of giving and receiving help within families ...
> were treated as *unremarkable* experiences by many people who talked
> to us. They were seen as a characteristic part of family life. They form
> part of peoples' image of what constitutes 'a family'. (p. 163)

They point out that the conditions for developing commitments within families, and the community at large, are set in childhood. The boys were all developing such commitments. Yet, to fully understand what family life is like, we must listen hard to children, and not make assumptions about the commonalties within or between families. As one boy put it when he wrote to Carolyn after talking to her.

[All families] are different in some ways and the same in others.

Thinking Points

- In this chapter, the experiences of children who live in families where parents have multiple commitments have become visible. Think about a family you know, in which parents have multiple commitments to work and caring, and consider the positive contributions the children make to the life of the family.

- Make a list of the advantages gained by children living in families where parents have multiple commitments for work and caring. What functions does the family serve for these children, such as meeting their needs for security, identity, and so on?

- Consider the reasons why issues facing children whose parents have multiple commitments are important for understanding any child's family life. What does understanding their experiences tell us about the importance for children of maintaining a private and a public boundary around their families?

Chapter 4

Dual Career Families

Suzan Lewis, Judith Sixsmith and Carolyn Kagan

Introduction

Many children living in two parent families have both parents in employment, or seeking employment. Dual earner families have a weekly income estimated to be 45 per cent higher than that in single earner families (Graham, 1993). Few families can afford to live on one income, even if they wished to do so. However, while social policy in most European states is based on the dual earner family as the norm, policy in the UK continues to assume a male breadwinner/female homemaker model (Brannen, Meszaros, Moss and Poland, 1994). For example, there is no statutory entitlement to family leave from work to care for a sick child: this assumes a parent (mother) at home or whose income is non-essential for the family and reflects an ambivalence among policy-makers about mothers of young children working outside the home.

This ambivalence has also been reflected in research on families and employment. For example, there is a substantial literature comparing children of employed and non-employed mothers, much of which was based, at least initially, on an assumption that maternal employment may have a negative impact on young children. However, no consistent differences have been found among children solely on the basis of maternal employment status (Hoffman, 1989). More recent research suggests that parents' (both mothers and fathers) experiences of work, rather than their employment status as such, may impact on children's behaviour (McEwen and Barling, 1993). Little attention has been paid, however, to children's own accounts of their day-to-day experiences in relation to their parents' work.

One variant of the dual earner family is the dual career family in which both partners pursue demanding careers and also raise children. The stressors as well as the satisfactions associated with this lifestyle for parents are well documented (Lewis and Cooper, 1987, 1988), but the impact of parents' careers on family life has mostly been considered from an adult's perspective, overlooking the children's own viewpoint. In this chapter, the experience of dual career family life is explored through the reflections of two children, Thomas aged 8, and Jill aged 15, both of whom have parents involved in demanding and often pressurized careers. Of course, some of other children discussed in other chapters also live in dual earner families, although this was not the focus of their interviews.

Children's Reflections

The two children who took part in the research both enjoyed the experience of being interviewed. Once they had settled down to thinking and talking about their families, they were able to articulate their feelings and experiences. Getting the children to compare their own family with friends' families helped them to clarify their thoughts on their own family situation. Neither of the children saw their families as being different from those of their friends or other families that they knew. When asked if their friends' parents all worked it emerged that this was not a significant factor in terms of the ways in which they understood family life:

> *Interviewer*: Are they like your friends' families, your family?
> *Jill*: Yes, more or less.
> *Interviewer*: Most of your friends' parents?
> *Jill*: Yes, most of them work.
> *Interviewer*: Do you have any friends whose parents don't work?
> *Jill*: Erm, not sure, don't really talk about it that much.

For Thomas, other differences between his family and his friends' families are much more obvious than their parents' occupations and working patterns:

> [My family is] different from friends' families because Jalal's believe in
> Hindu, Tim believes in God and Jesus.

It becomes clear through the children's comments that the fulltime presence of mother at home is not a prerequisite for positive mothering, as Thomas says:

> My mum is nice, and short, and she smiles a lot and she always looks
> on the bright side of life [*sings*] da da da da da da da da da and it's a bit
> silly sometimes because when like I'm really like, I can't . . because
> I'm being bullied, she just goes 'Just ignore him' . . . She's got lots of
> friends and she used to play sports but she tore a muscle in her leg
> in April and she can't do sports. She likes reading and writing and
> she's really nice and she likes thinking . . and helping people, and she
> loves strew and chilli.

Part of the reason that the children do not feel deprived if their parents are not always present is that they both think of their family in wider terms than just their mother and father. Thomas describes his family as comprising his mum and dad, his grandparents, his aunties and uncles and cousins, including even those members of the family who live in Australia and have very little contact with him on an everyday basis. Jill talks about her brother:

> We used to sort of come home from school together and watch telly together, but he's at college now so we don't see so much of each other.

Learning About the World of Work

The knowledge that children develop about their parents' jobs may be regarded as the beginning of the process of socialization about work, possibly determining future attitudes to work (Abramovitch and Johnson, 1992). Both children had some understanding of their parents' work. Thomas does not think he knows a great deal about their jobs, but he understands some of what they entail:

> My dad works as a gerontologist . . my mum works as a psychologist . . I don't know much about it . . she reads . . . she teaches a lot.

Jill understands more about her mother's jobs than her father's, because nurses are often encountered in everyday life, and because her mother talks to her more about her work which makes it appear more interesting:

> *Jill*: [Mum is] a nurse . . [Dad] sells computer assisted power stations . . something like that . . . she sometimes talks about her patients.
> *Interviewer*: And what about your dad? Does he talk to you [about work]?
> *Jill*: Not that much. It's not very interesting.

Much of the children's knowledge derived from their parents' willingness to include them in their working life. Thomas would sometimes visit both his dad's and his mum's workplace. From this he constructed a partial understanding of the job they performed and the places where they were employed:

> [My mum] she's got lots of friends [at work] . . and she's got a student called Samuel who's got a disease but he's a nice friend, he's always nice. And she's got two cafes, one for students and one for everybody . . She thinks I know the way and she leaves me and I say 'Mum!' and she comes back and gets me . . it's a nice warm place.

The children also learn about other aspects of the world of work from their parents. For example, Thomas learned about the dress codes of certain types of work:

[Dad's] a humorous fellow . . . he's usually smart when he goes to work, very posh, tie, shirt, suit and polished shoes. Well my mum doesn't go to work smart. She just likes to wear ordinary clothes.

Both children formed impressions about the positive and negative aspects of the work in which their parents were engaged, and about how their parents felt about their work. Thomas thinks that his parents enjoy their work and that this is important to them, although he also says that sometimes they come home in a bad mood or very tired from their work. Jill also recognizes that her mother's work can be stressful at times, but she says that her mother usually focuses on the positive aspects of her work so she is more aware of these:

Interviewer: Do you think your mother's job is stressful?
Jill: Yeah . . she gets these like old women coming in and complaining about their eye drops or whatever . . and they've got like little babies in with eye problems and stuff.
Interviewer: It must be a bit upsetting sometimes?
Jill: Well, she finds it good, like when old women can see again and they start saying how wonderful it is.

Work and Family Boundaries

Dual career parents often report difficulties in managing the boundaries between work and family and worry that work spilling over into family time may be detrimental (Lewis and Cooper, 1989). This suggests an assumption that children should be protected from the real world of work. The two children in this study are aware of permeable boundaries between home and work but do not always see this as a problem. Thomas is amused that his parents sometimes talk about their work in family time, using language he does not understand:

Well the funniest thing about me mum and dad's work is that we're in cafes and mum and dad are like speaking in a foreign language but it's just them using long words like 'sophisticated children should be crystallized if you observed them to . . .' so and on and on and on and on, long, long words, really long ones . . I used to laugh when they did that [*laughs*].

He accepts that his father will not have time to talk to him while he is at work, although it took him a little while to learn this:

[When dad's at work] he usually . . he doesn't look after me because his room is very small and cramped, it's a very small place . . . and it's cramped with books and computers and usually I'm not allowed in there. Catherine [his secretary] looks after me and I usually draw pictures . . I don't mind, I don't mind really because the first time I minded and the second time I minded and the third time I minded, but the fourth time I got used to it, I just got used to it. Usually [daddy says] 'Oh I've got things to do . . I've got a meeting' and I usually go to mum's work.

Thomas appreciates that his parents sometimes bring work home in the evenings and at weekends. He does hint, however, that his mother's working at home may prevent him having friends round:

> *Interviewer*: What do you do with your friends?
> *Thomas*: Invite them round, but my mummy doesn't want me to, she usually says, 'I'm sorry, they can't come round today.'
> *Interviewer*: Why do you think she says that?
> *Thomas*: Because she doesn't want me to.

Jill also feels that her mother's long hours sometimes prevented her and her brother from taking part in certain activities when they were younger:

> It's just if we have to go out at night and she's working late or whatever, or both parents are busy . . there's no-one to take you. That's the only difficulty really.

The children are clear, however, that they see the benefits of both their parents working as outweighing the drawbacks, and perceived advantages are considered next.

Independence

Both children recognize that their parents' enjoyment of their work is a positive thing for family life. Jill articulates the advantage in terms of both parents having independence, which she sees as very important. Although she does not talk about any families she knows where the mother is a fulltime homemaker, she nevertheless has a very negative view of what this might be like for a woman:

> It's good because like both my parents have got careers and stuff. It's not like one's stuck at home all day . . . because they are both sort of independent of each other really . . they don't depend on each other.

Jill values independence highly and also sees the advantage of being able to be independent herself, and of opportunities to learn to be independent, which she feels she might not have if her parents were always at home.

Security and Material Advantages

One advantage of living in a dual career family, which Thomas reveals, is a strong sense of security which he relates to financial stability. In addition, he is quite clear about the material advantages of having two employed parents:

> *Interviewer*: What difference does your mum and dad's work make to your life?
> *Thomas*: That's a hard one . . it makes my life easier because they get a lot of money so they can get food.

and

> *Interviewer*: Do you ever wish that your mummy or your daddy didn't have to go to work?
> *Thomas*: No. I like them to go to work . . . they get a lot of money to keep our house . . we could like go to the pictures . . I get pocket money . . . they get a lot of money and we've got two computers in the house and a CD player.

From the child's perspective, family security and material privilege go hand in hand with parents holding down successful careers.

Forming Relationships with Other Adults

Having both parents in employment inevitably means that children are looked after in a wide variety of child-care arrangements encompassing other adult carers such as family members, family friends and child-care professionals. Both children mentioned the advantages of being able to form relationships with other adults and the benefits they have gained through widened social horizons. Children's capacity to benefit from the opportunities for relationships and experiences which alternative child-care arrangements offer should not be underestimated:

> *Jill*: I had a childminder for a bit, and she used to pick me up [from school] and then stay at home for about an hour or so until my mum got back.
> *Interviewer*: Were you happy with her?
> *Jill*: Yeah. She used to play with me . . . and I think she enjoyed it more because she was getting paid.

Thomas also talked about the child-care arrangements he experienced which involved being picked up from school twice a week by a family friend and her daughter. As an only child, this was important in placing him in regular close contact with one of his many friends. In terms of developing independent friendships, new adult friends are made in the parents' workplaces as well as through child-care arrangements. For example, Thomas regards his father's secretary and his mother's colleagues as friends.

Being separated from their parents is not always a totally positive experience for the children, but neither is it totally negative. For example, Thomas recognizes that there is a trade-off between cuddles from his parents and being spoilt by his grandma when his parents are away:

> *Interviewer*: Sometimes you have to go to other people's to be looked after.
> *Thomas*: Yeah . . it's quite sad in some ways because my mummy and daddy go away. Like my mummy's going away for quite a long time and my daddy's going away for five days, but it's also happy because my grandma's coming to look after me . . . I'll miss cuddling together and waking up in the mornings and seeing them but my grandma spoils me and I'll probably get lots of videos, I'll probably see lots of videos, we'll probably get loads of videos, but we probably won't tell [mum]!

Time for Themselves

Dual career families are widely berated by the media in Britain for creating 'latch-key children', who are obliged, by their parents' commitments, to return from school to an empty house. However, neither Thomas or Jill regard themselves as 'latch-key kids.' Thomas understands what support there is. His parents have built up a secure network of alternative support and he understands that a wide range of possible arrangements have been made for his care:

> [My dad] I think he's fulltime so I usually expect him to be . . I usually expect him not to pick me up. My mum goes halftime, she usually picks me from school . . erm I think this is the last week that my mum's friend's picking me up.

> Grandma, she takes me out to parks and meets me when my mum's not there . . Aunty Shirley sometimes looks after me . . not all the time, usually when me grandma and granddad can't look after me . . I go to Aunty Shirley's house. In a few weeks time my grandma's coming to my house [she's going to] look after me because my mum and dad are away on business.

> Sarah [mum's friend] and my friend Esther [meet me from school]. On Mondays I have French lessons and then we go back and watch 'Genie From Down Under' and then after that we go to piano lessons.

Far from viewing herself as a latch-key child, Jill talks of the advantages of coming home and having the house to herself. Solberg (1990) refers to the positive aspects of coming home to a vacant house and Jill's account illustrates this point, showing how she misses the time to herself when her mother is there:

> When my mum's got a day off or whatever, when I come home she's there. Whatever I do she knows what I'm doing [*laughs*] . . . [When mum's not in] you can have loads to eat without her complaining, can relax in front of the telly or get some work done . . . yeah, so it's better that way.

Time Together

Some of the most pressing issues for dual career parents concern the management of time (Lewis and Cooper, 1989). Many parents are concerned about the numerous demands on their time, and often respond by ensuring that they spend what has been termed 'quality time' (Hoffman, 1989) with their children. Thomas echoes these concerns. He feels that he would sometimes like more time with his parents, especially his dad:

> My dad's always away on business . . it's not fair, I don't usually get see him . . I'd like to see him more often.

and

> I don't like it when he comes home [from work] at seven or eight. I don't like it when he comes home at eight, I like seven because we've got two more hours and that's quite nice . . we play . . I play dinosaurs a lot, he keeps on telling me about his interviewing . . and now I'm being interviewed!

Jill feels that this is less of a concern to her as an adolescent:

> [Mum] sometimes works until about half nine or ten, but it doesn't matter. I'm still up then anyway.

Scarcity of time makes the family appreciate the time they do have together. For example, Thomas greatly values time he does spend with his parents, and, though he has expressed some reservations abut how much time they actually have together, they undoubtedly have a secure and happy relationship, built around mutual sharing of interests and family activities:

> Dad likes to play football with me and cricket with me and sports with me . . he likes every sport. He likes making this tape that I'm doing

.. a tape that I'm making on the CD player with all dance music on .. like Power Rangers, Village People, That's What I Call Music, the Flintstones, dance music .. and he doesn't like taking Joe out .. Joe's the dog. He likes taking me out with him, but he doesn't like taking him out if I'm not going .. we go round the block .. dad takes me out .. swimming, sometimes the arcades, usually swimming . . . Dad's got cool records like David Bowie.

Thomas: With my mum we go to erm with my mum we go to a friend's house .. [We] usually go there, and we usually go to the library, but sometimes we just sit down in the study and just read.
Interviewer: Just you and your mum together?
Thomas: Yeah sometimes, sometimes we just look out at the cars going by in the dark as it's getting darker. I remember once when I had lots of books by the side of me and I read them all in a few minutes and I was waiting for my tea and I just liked staring out the window and it kept being the same yellow car coming round and round and round and I kept seeing it.
Interviewer: That sounds quite nice.
Thomas: Yeah.

Gender

Parents model gender roles for their children. Although rarely totally egalitarian, dual career parents, more often than single earner parents, deviate from the traditional gendered division of domestic labour. This can reduce the stress of the double burden of paid and unpaid work experienced by many women in dual earner households (Hochschild, 1989). Jill's parents both contribute to the domestic work and she recognizes that both her mother and father have a great deal of domestic as well as paid work:

[Dad] does sort of a load of work round the house as well, so he's always tired.

Children may become more involved in family work if both parents are employed for much of the time, but this is not necessarily the case. Jill feels that she should help more around the house, and that her parents would like her to do so, but admits that she does not:

Interviewer: How do you feel when she [your mother] is tired?
Jill: I feel sorry for her.
Interviewer: So do you help her a bit more?
Jill: Not really, no [*laughs*]. I should do but I don't really.

Interviewer: Do you feel you should be helping your dad too?
Jill: Um yeah. I don't do that much to help and I should do.

She is quite open about her brother doing more housework than she does, particularly in terms of keeping their own bedrooms tidy:

Jill: He does help more than me.
Interviewer: Your brother does?
Jill: Yeah, I sort of try and get out of it.

Although traditional gender roles are blurred in Jill's family, with regard to domestic work, she is nevertheless aware of gender differences in the emotional support she receives from her parents:

Jill: We all sort of tell each other our problems .. can talk to our parents .. can talk to my mother about anything really.
Interviewer: And your dad?
Jill: Erm, not so much as my mum I don't think, but I could do.
Interviewer: Is it because he's busier?
Jill: No, dad, he's a male. He's dad.

Children's Own Aspirations

Children's future aspirations are partly determined by their childhood experiences of family life. For girls, simply having an employed mother does not guarantee that they will aspire to a career and family life (Gilbert and Dancer, 1992). There is some evidence that girls from more egalitarian families are more likely to aspire to both, while those whose mothers struggle to combine career and family with little support from their partners are more likely to believe that it will be necessary to make choices between career and family (Gilbert and Dancer, 1992). Jill thinks that she will be able to combine both career and family in the same way that her mother has done, that is by having a career break:

Jill: I would want to be sort of independent really.
Interviewer: What do you think you might do if you were to have children, do you think you might perhaps go back to work straight away?
Jill: No .. I don't know, it would depend on what job I've got. I'd rather take sort of take a few years off . . . see them growing up.

She is aware, however, that this will depend on the conditions of the occupation and job she chooses, and knows that having both is not always possible for all women:

It depends what I'll be doing . . I'd like to take the time off, but it depends if I can . . I'd probably get bored staying at home all day.

Thomas's aspirations as an 8-year-old are more idealistic:

Interviewer: What would you like your family to be like when you grow up?
Thomas: My family . . richer so we could have a house in the country . . . just like we are now with a bigger garden than we've got now, and a tree-house for the children . . . even from an orphanage, two boys and two girls, my family would be strict and it wouldn't be strict, just like a normal family.

Dislikes

When we asked the children what they disliked about their family life, they both had strong views. However, the dislikes were about aspects of family life that were unrelated to the dual career family lifestyle. Thomas expressed some dislike of family rules:

I don't like . . My dad can get very strict sometimes . . I might have a little argument and he says, 'Get into your bedroom Thomas.' And I'm sometimes a bit naughty and my mum and my dad send me to my room and I just play . . . and then come back and say, 'I'm sorry'.

[On rules about watching television] I'm only allowed to watch it on evenings, Saturday mornings and Sunday mornings. Sometimes on Saturday morning I go to the cinema club and see lots of pictures.

And I have to go to bed at half past eight. I don't think my best . . one of my friends, Jalal, does this, but he says he goes to bed at 10 o'clock! But he goes to bed at 9 o'clock.

Jill, on the other hand, discussed sibling rivalry and a feeling that her brother was her parents' favourite:

Jill: My parents like go to his parents' evenings [at school] and he gets B in his reports and mine are just like awful.
Interviewer: How sickening.
Jill: Yeah, exactly.
Interviewer: They come back and talk about it do they?
Jill: Yeah, they go on about how wonderful he is and how I should work hard like him and all that.

She also reiterates her concern about independence, which she seems to feel she has to fight for more than her brother:

Jill: They give my brother more freedom, let him do more.
Interviewer: Let him go out more?
Jill: Well he doesn't really go out that much. He's just allowed more freedom. He's just allowed more freedom in everything he does really. That's probably because he's a bit older, but I'm sure he never got this [restriction] when he was my age.

The emotional ups and downs of family life are plainly evident in both children's accounts, just as they are in the accounts of most of the children in other chapters within this book.

Dual Career Family Life: Children's Perspectives

The children we spoke to do not feel that they are different because both their parents are employed outside the home and have demanding careers. This is taken for granted as the norm. When pressed, they can see some problems that this brings, but they are all much more aware of the advantages, and they would not prefer one parent to be at home full time.

The problems that they do see are about parents working long or irregular hours, particularly lack of time with parents if they work in the evenings. However, this is not too great a problem for these children because both mothers have accommodated their work in some way to make time for children. In this respect, they are typical of many dual career families. In some cases it is the father who makes these accommodations, especially if the mother is the higher earner, but this is more unusual. It would be interesting to talk to children in mother breadwinner dual earner families, to see of this, too, is accepted as the norm, and how they feel about their parents' roles.

Both Thomas' and Jill's mothers work in occupations where it is possible to reduce working time to make more time for their children, although this may be at some cost, ultimately, in terms of career advancement, income and pensions. Other parents are not able to do this, either because two fulltime incomes are required or because they work in less flexible occupations. Furthermore, many jobs require employees to work more than fulltime hours, putting in extra time to demonstrate 'commitment' (Lewis and Taylor, forthcoming), despite the fact that long hours may be inefficient and unproductive. However, the feeling of many parents — that it is necessary to be seen to be working long hours — is unlikely to change until employers recognize the counterproductive nature of the long hours culture, both for family life and for employing organizations. The current economic climate with downsizing, restructuring and widespread job insecurity cause many parents to feel compelled to work long hours and this can create considerable conflict and feelings of guilt for parents of young children (Lewis and Cooper, 1989).

We have seen in this chapter how important it is for the children to feel

63

secure in their home life. We now need to know more about how children perceive the stress caused by job insecurity for many parents. Parents who are both in demanding careers requiring long hours have been described as 'work rich' (Brannen *et al*, 1994). Others are 'work poor' with both parents unemployed or underemployed. We also need to know more about how children experience family life in families where economic hardship may be exacerbated by parental employment frustrations.

For the children we interviewed, the overall experience of living in a dual career family is positive. They are aware that their parents make, or have made, elaborate arrangements for their care and appreciate quality time that they spend with them. Looking through children's eyes, we see that adult concepts such as latch-key children and spillover of work into family time can, at least in some circumstances, be constructed by children not as problems, but as opportunities to be independent and to develop relationships with other adults. The children have occasion to learn about and even experience their parents' work which can enrich their lives and prepare them for their own employment choices. The recently evolved tradition of having a 'Take your daughters to work day' is based on the assumption that this will help girls to recognize the wide range of jobs which women can do and hence to broaden their experiences and aspirations. It can be argued that all children can benefit from breaking down the boundaries between work and family and from opportunities to learn about the world of work in the most natural way, through gaining an insight into their own parents' working lives. However, not all occupations and workplaces are as children-friendly as Thomas' parents' workplaces appear to be. For example, Jill knows virtually nothing about her father's work, which retains a mystique and which consequently limits the boundaries of her aspirations.

It is clear that dual career parents and their children have much to gain from this lifestyle. Nevertheless policy-makers need to recognize that male breadwinner and female homemaker families are now the exception to the norm and that dual earner families need support. Child-care provisions and programmes for after-school and school holiday care can all help in the management of work and family. Equally important, however, especially from the children's perspectives, are parents' needs for time to lead a balanced life, including time to spend with the families. Social policies (such as family leave to care for a sick child) are useful and can help to ensure that parents have time for children in a crisis. In addition, employer 'family-friendly' policies, such as flexitime, or part-time work with pro rata benefits, can help parents to manage multiple demands. However, the take up of family-friendly policies, especially by men, remains limited at present because employees are often valued according to how much time they spend at the workplace, and because of a climate of job insecurity. If we really value children, we have to challenge basic organizational cultures and norms by considering children's perspectives on family life as important inputs to their parents' employment conditions.

Thinking points

• What factors influence the quality of life in the dual career family from the child's perspective? Talk to a dual career couple to find out what they feel about how their work influences family life. Note any similarities or differences between the perspectives of adults and children.

• What are the components of an idealized version of dual career family life? What parts of family life do you feel are most vulnerable when both parents have careers? Review your answers to these questions and think about what supports are required to ensure dual career couples can overcome obstacles.

• Find out about the policies relating to family life in your own workplace, or college. To what extent are these policies family-friendly? What policy and practical recommendations could be made to further facilitate the well-being of dual career families who are connected with that organization? Can you put your recommendations forward to anyone in a position to bring about change?

Chapter 5

Split Family Life

Michele Moore and Sarah Beazley

Introduction

In this chapter, children's responses to their situation in split families are explored with a view to illustrating their perspective on the topical question of how children cope when their parents live separately. The percentage of children living with both parents is known to be in steady decline (Barnados Today, 1994). Many myths about the disadvantages of living in a split family, which Morris (1992) enabled single mothers to refute, are also challenged by children. The children interviewed for this chapter do not dwell on inadequacies of the split family situation. Instead, they focus on a wide range of supports that are made available to them, and show themselves immensely flexible in the face of alternatives to family life where both parents live together. They can point out difficulties of family life when parents live separately, but do not identify themselves as living in a family which is any less satisfactory, or enabling, to that enjoyed by children whose parents do not live apart. This observation leads us to query, then, why it is so often assumed that family life is problematic when parents split up, and that children are invariably thrown into a second best situation (Wallerstein and Blakeslee, 1989; Alanen, 1992; Whithead, 1993). This is important because children coping well with split family life are made vulnerable if they continually have to contend with the myth that family life is only truly adequate when two parents live together. We know there can be problems, but there are also strengths, in split family life (Richards and Schmiege, 1993).

The two girls interviewed for this chapter are from greatly differing backgrounds, experiences and situations. At the time of the interviews, Julie, aged 5, had recently witnessed a stressful breakdown in her parents' relationship. Her father had left the family home in acrimonious style several months before she took part in the study. She was living with her mother and 2-year-old brother Thomas in a village outside a large business town in the south east of England. Emily, aged 7, lived in a large north eastern town, part week with her mother, her mother's partner, their daughter, and her mother's partner's daughter, and the rest of the week alone with her father. She had been accustomed to these arrangements for most of her life. At the time of Emily's interview, the relationship between her two parents was amicable, whereas between Julie's there was animosity. Julie was interviewed alone by the first author, and Emily was interviewed by both chapter authors together.

As young children living in split families, Julie and Emily's views have indefinite status. On the one hand, their understandings and reactions are, as Emily acknowledges, immature and probably based on fragmented knowledge of the ins and outs of their family circumstances. On the other, however, they both worked hard to provide the fullest possible explanations of their situations and were very keen to have their input taken seriously.

It is worth saying that there is no intention to either recycle negative images of split family life in this chapter, or to promote a particularly favourable impression, as such motivations would undoubtedly propel many other single parent families and their children into feelings of inadequacy. The aim is simply to present the reflections of two children who live in split families from their own point of view as a resource for further consideration and discussion. The children's own reflections on their very different experiences of split family life are much more powerful and revealing than indirect reporting on their situations and so we will immediately bring these to the front of the discussion.

Children's Reflections

Is Split Family Life a Problem?

Do children living in split families see their situation as a problem? When asked what it is like to be in her family Julie said, 'Nice,' and was able to explain, 'Nice because I've got lots of friends'. She appeared to find surrogate family through supportive friends in the event of her parents separating. So we might consider whether assumed deficiencies when parents decide to live apart can be compensated through the willingness of other people the child has contact with to provide back up. Emily, who has longer experience of her parents living separately, reserves judgment on split family life, however, saying:

> I don't know, I'm not quite sure yet. I'll probably be able to tell you
> that when I'm older .. I can't give the answer till when I'm older.

Either way, the important point is that both children signal the danger of assuming that split family life is problematic.

A strong feature of the children's reflections is that they both define their family very widely, and in doing so reveal themselves to be perfectly capable of understanding and managing the complexities of their respective situations. It is worth taking a look at their open-mindedness, in this respect, for each child in turn.

Michele Moore and Sarah Beazley

A Wide Range of Supports

Julie described a range of people in response to the issue of 'Who is in your family?'. Listed in the order in which she identified them, Julie included:

> mummy
> Thomas [brother]
> me
> daddy
> granddad
> great granddad
> great granny
> Greg, 'he's my friend'
> Janey, 'she's my friend'
> Phillipa, 'she's only five'
> Ella, 'she's Phillipa's sister'
> Andrea and Tim, 'Phillipa's daddy' [and mother]

Although Julie included all of these people in the account of who is in her family, she was precisely able to indicate those who are actually relatives and those who are not. Evidently, then, young children need not restrict their view of who constitutes their family to relations alone, and can extend their sights to include a range of other people who fulfil important roles in their lives. Neither do they confine their view of the family to those who live with them. It is interesting to note that non-relatives who are included in Julie's view of her family all play key roles in helping to sustain both her family and home life, and she fully appreciates the extent of this. Greg and Janey, for example, a couple who are friends of Julie's mother, offer much that Julie identifies as beyond friendship. Though she knows they are her friends she embraces them as family because of the things they do for her:

> *Interviewer*: How is Greg in your family?
> *Julie*: He gives me Smarties . . . he's my friend.
> *Interviewer*: He is your friend isn't he . . . do you want to put him in [your family picture] then?
> *Julie*: Yes, next to great-granny because he's good at making people better because . . he makes me go better with special medicine if I hurt myself . . . when I have growing pains he's nice.

Many of the roles Greg and Janey play in Julie's life are those which parents take on, but in the absence of one parent it is helpful to take a wider range view of who can fulfil parental responsibilities when families are split:

> *Interviewer*: What sort of things do you do with Greg?
> *Julie*: Reading . . . he picks me up from school . . . he does 'jumble words' with me. [homework]

Interviewer: What do you do with Janey?
Julie: She picks me up from school and she treats me, and she buys me sweeties and I sleep at her house sometimes . . . we stay at Janey's a lot.

Julie did not randomly include any person she knew as a member of her family. Rather she carefully selected those who took on roles traditionally associated with parenting and home-making. Other friends identified as part of the family picture are those who also help to provide a home when her mother has to work nights:

Interviewer: Who else is in your family?
Julie: Phillipa. Well she lives in Chanbury and I'm going to stay with her tomorrow.
Interviewer: Right.
Julie: For three weeks.
Interviewer: For three weeks are you? Do you want to draw Phillipa then?
Julie: Yeah, Phillipa.
interviewer: Is Phillipa a grown-up person?
Julie: No she's only 5 . . . and her sister, her sister is 3.
Interviewer: Is there anyone else in your family, or have we done all those?
Julie: Ella, Andrea and Tim. [Phillipa's sister and parents]

Julie conceives of many people who are important allies in her life as family, and in doing so, alerts us to the capacities children may have for recognizing and accepting a wide range of supports when their parents live apart. She has a robust sense of belonging to a family unit even though her parents are separated.

Emily expanded her definition of who her family is made up of in the same broad manner. The people she included during the course of the interview were not all relatives. Emily was able to identify non-relatives. She also fully explained why some people whom onlookers might regard as family members were not included in her picture of her family. Thus Emily's picture of her family comprised:

my mum
my dad
my mum's sister, Rachel
my Uncle Jacks. I've got two Uncle Jacks. One which is my daddy's
    younger brother and one which is my mummy's big brother
I've got Richard [half-brother]
my nanna
Hanna . . . she's quite a small baby . . . she acts as if she's my big
    sister, but I'm her big sister [half-sister]

> Barry . . . my mum's boyfriend. He's not really . . I've . . haven't really
> got his blood . . [not] blood relative
> mummy's mummy
> daddy's mummy
> and Jim and my big uncle and his big brother

> I won't put in Meg, my little brother's mummy, because well she's not
> really part of our family. Not as much as she's not really a blood
> relative, neither is Rosie, so I'm not really going to put her . . . Rosie,
> she's my step-sister.

> my Poppops is my grandpa
> I've got two great grandmas
> uncle John, uncle Michael
> lots of [family] have died, like my Aunty Pamela
> some people I haven't even met like cousins

Both children, whose accounts are presented here, have a clear view of who
they include in their personal understandings of family, and the fact that their
parents live separately does not mean that either of them subsequently portrays themself as inadequately supported. They both ascribe family membership according to the roles people play, rather than to biological or legal
ties. Relatives who do not offer the child support are not a central part of
their family picture, whereas friends who do are included. 'Outsiders' are
'family' when they occupy some tangible role which affirms their identity as
a family member. Exploring this issue of who children consider to be in their
family offers fresh insights into their responses to split family life.

Children are Resourceful

Both Julie and Emily were realistic about relationships within the family, and
did not overlook the fact that there are emotional ups and downs associated
with family life. They both described siblings, for example, in mixed ways,
careful to point out both their good and bad points. Julie described her younger
brother as 'a bit fussy' and points out, 'He won't let me go on the swing . . .
but he's only two . . . [he's] a bit scribbly at drawing.' Even so, she offers him
encouragement and guidance:

> *Interviewer*: He is old isn't he great-granddad. Do you want to draw
> a picture of him Thomas?
> *Thomas*: Yes.
> *Interviewer*: OK then.
> *Julie*: Thomas you know a line? That's for a walking stick right? You
> know a line? And a little up right, down up there and a little tail . .
> great-granddad's walking stick.

The trials of their relationship as described by Julie do not seem unique to siblings in split families, and are notable for their ordinariness. We can see similar relationships between siblings in the chapter on traditional families and, indeed, in the accounts of most children with siblings reported throughout this book. Other testing aspects of life with a younger brother emerged:

> *Julie*: He kills fish because he splashed the water all around when yesterday my mum said I can tickle the frog. And do you know once my brother put a chick . . a rat, no, I mean a tissue paper, on my salad.

In contrast, the tensions Emily reveals in a different, though equally candid, description of problems with her brother might in part be better understood by addressing the dynamics of split family life. The only certainty here, as Emily reminds the interviewer, is that any assumptions are dangerous:

> *Emily*: [My half-brother] he's a bit shy he doesn't like going away from his mummy, he doesn't have to very often, he's never been away with his daddy or anything. He has been away with us but hardly ever. He's a bit of a mummy's boy.
> *Interviewer*: Do you two get on because you're very similar in age aren't you, but it doesn't mean you get on.
> *Emily*: We do.
> *Interviewer*: You do.
> *Emily*: He often doesn't want to come and see us, because of his mummy.
> *Interviewer*: What do you like about him?
> *Emily*: I don't know I just like him.
> *Interviewer*: Do you like doing the same sort of things?
> *Emily*: Sometimes we do, sometimes we don't.

In these comments, Emily has shown the capacity to function as a fully fledged sister even in a multiple split family situation where some siblings live apart and others live together. She has the ability to recognize the dilemmas that the situation presents for her brother, and sufficient adeptness to build a caring relationship with him. She is ready to recognize different pressures on individual members of her family, just as, even from an extremely young age, she finds her younger half-sister responds to her needs:

> *Emily*: My Hanna, my little sister is really cute and says 'What's the matter?'
> *Interviewer*: She tries to comfort you does she?
> *Emily*: Yeah. If I lie on the arm chair or the sofa this is what I get, 'shush shush, go to sleep you,' and then she lifts up my jumper and licks my back.
> *Interviewer*: Is she trying to make you feel better?
> *Emily*: It's when I lie down on the chair . . . and even if I'm not, even

if I'm just lying down underneath a blanket, watching the TV, she'll start jumping on me then 'shush shush I'm going to sleep you,' and sometimes she'll get a book and pretend to read it . . . well she pretends. She says she is. Pretends to read it but she doesn't. I read things to her.

These extracts remind us to avoid seeing children's needs only in terms of the support adults can offer. The two brothers who are the focus of Julie and Emily's reflections are clearly on the receiving end of some considerable empathy from their sisters. Hanna (who Emily has said, is 'only a small baby') is clearly ready to show patience and to empathize with her sister. From what the children say, it seems unnecessary to view the adequacies of split families only in relation to what parents themselves bring to a child's situation. As we see, children help each other out too. And, in addition, children freely show themselves to be mindful of support they can give to adults:

> *Interviewer*: What sort of little girl are you?
> *Julie*: Nice.
> *Interviewer*: Nice yeah, why are you nice?
> *Julie*: Because . . help mummy, help tidy up.
> *Interviewer*: Yes, anything else?
> *Julie*: Help mummy find slugs in the garden . . . help mummy hoover.

and similarly,

> *Julie*: She's very nice great-grandma.
> *Interviewer*: Is she?
> *Julie*: Granny, she's got a lot of tales.
> *Interviewer*: What else, what else makes her nice?
> *Julie*: She gives me sweeties, and she does . . . well she does . . . she umm . . sometimes she phones us and she's ill and my mum speaks to her and me, we have to speak loud because she's very quiet.
> *Interviewer*: Oh right.
> *Julie*: Yeah, we have to speak loud.

Like Emily at age 7, Julie at 5 is capable of taking the needs of other people into account and does not seem to need two parents living together to help her do this. Both children show a capacity to bring complementary skills to their own situation, such as sharing tasks and responsibilities for other family members.

Practical Matters

Both Julie and Emily explore aspects of their family situation which raise practical difficulties. They both mentioned money matters and Julie, in particular, cannot separate her awareness of new financial family difficulties from the way in which she describes her father:

> *Interviewer*: What's your daddy like?
> *Julie*: Naughty.
> *Interviewer*: Is he naughty? Why do you think he's naughty?
> *Julie*: Because he won't pay the bills . . . he won't pay the mortgage.
> *Interviewer*: Anything else?
> *Julie*: He didn't buy me new shoes . . . he buys me ice-cream.

Emily realizes there are money problems, but views these as a fact of life saying:

> She's poor, my mum is, my dad is rich, well my dad is rich to my mummy, anyway . . . but I don't mind.

At the same time, both children show they do find it hard to shoulder some aspects of their split family situation. Julie briefly describes her difficulties:

> *Interviewer*: And you sometimes go to your daddy's home don't you?
> *Julie*: Yep.
> *Interviewer*: What's his home like?
> *Julie*: Bit stinky because his girlfriend smokes.
> *Interviewer*: Oh dear.
> *Julie*: Ugh. It makes me sick. It makes me feel sick.

Emily has had rather longer to come to terms with her split family life but still indicates some disquiet, particularly when she makes it plain that her separated parents find some difficulty orchestrating her movements:

> *Interviewer*: You said before that sometimes you lived [with daddy] and sometimes you lived [with mummy].
> *Emily*: Yes.
> *Interviewer*: So tell us a bit more about that.
> *Emily*: OK. Well I go to my mum's, stay there a week, no four days a week, I go to my dad three days a week. Sometimes my daddy swaps it round a bit and my mummy gets a bit cross, but sometimes my mummy swaps it round a bit and my daddy gets cross.

It transpires that this is a difficult thing to talk about:

> *Interviewer*: Emily, could you tell us a bit what it's like living in your family?
> *Emily*: *Stretched.*

> *Interviewer*: Stretched. What does stretched mean?
> *Emily*: I mean everybody is wanting to have me at the same time.
> *Interviewer*: Are they?
> *Emily*: Yes. My mummy is wanting to have me when my daddy wants to have me, my granny wants to have me when my nanna's having me. They all want to have me when they haven't got me.
> *Interviewer*: Oh, so how does that make you feel?
> *Emily*: I don't know . . my dad . . mummy gets very cross, because she thinks my daddy's not being fair, she think he's not paying his . . getting his . . getting not getting his share, she thinks that she's getting too much child care. She thinks that he ought to have some more. Because he hasn't had very much lately . .
> *Interviewer*: What do you think? You said what mummy thinks. What do you think?
> *Emily*: I don't know. [*long pause, pulls a face*]
> *Interviewer*: You're rolling your eyes about like you had a little thought in there . . [*no reply*]
> *Interviewer*: Not sure? [*no reply*]

Thus both children laid open a need for support to enable them to express and deal with concerns about the practical business of split family life. They know from experience that practical difficulties bring pressures, yet position themselves as having very little control over these matters:

> *Emily*: One thing I don't like about having lots of people . . . I never know who I'm going to be with when I go home from school. I never know who I'm going to be with at home time. My dad or my mum they never tell me.

Both children have shown ability to recognize their own feelings and to acknowledge advantages and disadvantages of their split family situation. Beyond this, however, whereas both children understood the split child-care arrangements that applied to them, they both presented their understanding of 'home' as principally located in one place.

What Makes Home?

Emily's notion of 'home' raises new questions, because, although she sees her family as spread across two households, it emerges that she does not regard her **home** as being in two places. This holds true for Julie too; although both children acknowledge their **family** is located in more than one place, and has to do with 'who I'm going to be with', they both perceive their **home** as fixed. The need for a single, fixed home is not flagged as problematic by the children. But as Emily unravelled her image of home her father, who had entered the room a few moments earlier, challenged her:

Interviewer: If you shut your eyes and imagine home, what comes to your mind, what words come into your mind?

Emily: Well my mum's house is bigger than the one we used to live in and my bedroom's quite big, I was going to swap rooms because there's three of us now my step-sister has come to live with us. So they're going to take the small room and we are going to take the big one.

Interviewer: You and Hanna are having the big one are you?

Emily: And Rosie.

Interviewer: . . . What's your home like?

Emily: Well it's got six rooms, There's the studio, the utility room, which is Barry's workshop, and there's my mum's studio, because she's an artist person. She keeps all her painting stuff in there, and bathroom, two bedrooms up in the attic and our sitting room. Daddy, stop laughing.

Dad: You've got two homes though.

Emily: Now I'll go on to daddy's one, add them up, four of them isn't there, four?

Dad: Six.

Emily: Bathroom, two bedrooms, kitchen, dining room, what else is there?

Dad: Front room.

Emily: Oh yes, that is our TV room and we call it front room.

When questioned by her father, Emily recognizes that she has two homes. When unchallenged, her mother's place is at the front of her mind when it comes to thinking about home, even though her mother's house is relatively new, and she refers in contrast to 'daddy's one'. For Emily, home is not simply a place of shared occupancy alongside either one parent. Julie also unhesitatingly expresses the view that her home is the place which she shares with her mother:

Interviewer: What pops into your head when you think about home?

Julie: Go to bed.

Interviewer: What else? What's it like your home?

Julie: Good.

Interviewer: It's good. Why is it good?

Julie: Because you play.

Interviewer: You play . . what else do you do at home?

Julie: And we do go on the swing, because we've got a swing in our garden.

Interviewer: . . Who lives in your home?

> *Julie*: Mummy and Thomas and me and that's all. My daddy doesn't live here any more because he left us.

The definition and boundaries of home given by Emily and Julie are primarily connected with mothers, and, in both instances, mothers are portrayed as the primary caretakers — at least (in Emily's case), portrayed in this way by the child. The link between mothers and home is not intended to be sanctified by such an observation, but it is automatically assumed by the two children interviewed here. We could, from this, start to address both what a current image of home indicates about a child's view of spilt family life, and how moving from an assumed link between family and home could enrich our understanding of what split family life means to them.

Strengths in Split Family Life

Although Julie and Emily can point to thorny aspects of their split family life, they do not dwell on these, and both freely describe enjoyable aspects without reference to barriers created by parents living separately. In doing so, they show a willingness to view their family and home situation in a positive way, even though they have pointed out problems with it. Emily, in particular, provides a convincing sense of family identity in her situation which an outsider might regard as having uncommonly complicated family boundaries. Her rendition of what it means to be a sister, for example, is unconcerned with the fact that one sister, Hanna, has the same mother as she (but not father) and the other sister, Rosie, is the daughter of her mother's live-in partner and so not biologically related to Emily:

> Me and my little sister have both got red dresses . . . me and Hanna have got two things the same, we've both got, we have both got red dresses we have both got green jumpers and green and blue jeans. My [hair is] a bit darker than hers, her hair is a bit lighter, and me and Rosie have got the same leggings and the same dresses. Me, Rosie and Hanna have all got the same dress it's a blue one with yellow flowers on.

In fact, when Emily contrasts her family situation with that of other children, including her half-brother who lives alone with one parent in less embroiled circumstances, she considers her own to offer distinct advantages:

> *Interviewer*: You're a bit more independent than [Richard] are you?
> *Emily*: Aha, I've been away with my granny, been away with lots of people without my mummy. Hanna has only been away with [my daddy] and to the chip shop.

Descriptions of family rituals, such as birthday celebrations, further nullify concern that the positive features of ordinary family life might be jeopardized for children in split families. We see that there is no need to focus on disadvantage even when families are under a range of pressures:

> *Interviewer*: Can you remember when it was your birthday in March? What did you do?
> *Julie*: We all put badges on . . 'Happy Birthday'.
> *Interviewer*: That's great isn't it?
> *Julie*: And we were making sweets and I could do the icing sugar!

> *Interviewer*: If there's a special occasion like if it's your birthday or something like that, what do you do?
> *Emily*: I try to tell everyone in advance so that they'll say 'Happy Birthday' . . . I try to invite everyone I can to my birthday party.
> *Interviewer*: Where do you have your birthday party?
> *Emily*: Often at home, last year, this year it was at home, last year it was at Pizza Hut, the year before one year I had this lovely birthday party, you should have seen the cake, it had twists of seaweed and you know those little chocolate bars you get with things, those were put on as rocks and stuff and there was fishy jelly sweets on top . . . and blue icing.

At least three positive elements of split family life are revealed by Julie and Emily: the ability to enjoy family life and kinship under pressure; an insight into, and care for, the perspectives of other family members; and a sense of belonging to a workable family unit. The two children, who are our focus here, engage with their respective situations in a variety of constructive ways, without submitting to the doctrine that their family situation is fundamentally flawed. While this, generally speaking, is the central observation in this chapter, we want to offer some reflections on the process of interviewing children about their experiences of split family life before summarizing our thoughts.

Methodological Issues

The approach taken in this chapter has been to present two children's reflections on split family life as providing viable insights. As emphasized elsewhere in this book, it is not assumed that the portrayals contain glimpses of what split family life might mean to other children. We simply aim to encourage readers to envisage a range of issues with which children in such a situation might be concerned.

In addition to broader deliberations on interviewing children for research, which are aired in our concluding chapter, it is worth briefly reflecting on special issues involving children in split families. In relation to this, an extremely powerful influence throughout the interviews with Julie and Emily was their sensitivity to the issue of public loyalty to both parents. Each child stopped talking when they felt their loyalties might appear divided, often insisting 'I don't know' as a strategy for opting out of particular explorations. They repeatedly cautioned us to 'Promise you're not going to tell anyone,' if they were choosing to 'spill the beans' (Hammersley and Atkinson, 1983). These tensions were evident in both interviews and especially in Emily's as she reacted most conspicuously to the presence or absence of a parent in the room:

> *Interviewer*: We don't know much about uncle Michael yet and the other uncle Jack.
> *Emily*: Stop laughing, Daddy.
> *Dad*: Not laughing at you, darling.
> *Emily*: Yes you are.
> *Dad*: Just laughing at our strange family.
> *Interviewer*: Can you say a bit about them?
> *Emily*: Not much.

and later:

> I'm glad he's gone now so that I can say that.

The reader will already have noticed various changes in the tone of comments quoted from the children's interviews. That this is so, and that the process of interviewing contributes to making this tone, is clearly illustrated through Emily's comments which show her awareness of both the intimacy usually attached to reflections on family matters and the delicacy of talking about such issues. Emily has no trouble recognizing the implicit expectations surrounding her position as an interviewee, and refuses to ignore these. About an hour and a half into the interview, for example, she breaks in, saying:

> *Emily*: . . . I'd like to ask you one question. What your book about?
> *Interviewer*: It's about what children think of their families.
> *Emily*: Oh.
> *Interviewer*: We told you that didn't we, in the beginning, didn't we? Do you need any more information about it? [*no reply*]
> *Interviewer*: You can always ask us, if you think of something else.
> *Emily*: OK. Daddy, every time I look at you, you seem to be laughing.

As researchers, we felt Emily was a more comfortable respondent when alone with the two interviewers. But we had no power to control the involvement of parents, and indeed feel this power rightly belonged to her supervising parent. Certainly these matters prompt further justification and elaboration of ways in which researchers and practitioners access children's views on ostensibly private matters.

Those who are privileged to access a child's reflections on split family life will have different views on which kinds of support are appropriate for individual children and the extent to which children of different ages should be encouraged to express themselves in relation to this. In debates about the fitness of split families, however, we need to repudiate negative assumptions about the extent to which children themselves can construct meaningful interpretations of their situation. In this chapter, we have tried to provide Julie and Emily with an opportunity to ward off such suspicions. If professionals and lay people alike are to touch on the impact that split family life has on a child, then we need to utilize each child's own reflections on their situation in our attempts to make sense of their experience and in advising others.

Split Family Life: Children's Perspectives

As Morris (1992) points out, there is a bias towards discussions of negative aspects of split family life in the literature. Images of impoverished, struggling and unhappy children continue to be familiar representations in the media. To some extent, these themes are reproduced here through concerns that the children have volunteered. It is, however, important to counter the tendency towards reinforcing oppressive aspects of split family life, and to be mindful of the positive pictures that the two children here have also freely identified in their experiences. The dominant impression society holds of children living in split families is an important aspect of their experience, and ill-informed or unrealistic ideas about the nature of children's experiences of split family living can only prove burdensome, to children, to their parents and to anyone who is concerned with children's participation in decisions concerning their well-being.

Julie and Emily both identify problems but also opportunities associated with split family life. Parents and professionals alike, need to engage as fully as possible with children's own reflections in any attempt to further understanding of their responses to the split — or, indeed, any other kind of 'different' — family situation. Children in split families need to have the same supports available to them as their peers in more traditional family situations and a critical source of this support is to be found in listening to the children's own reflections. There is need for acceptance, as we are reminded by both Julie and Emily, that adults often invest children with problems that they do not actually have.

At this juncture, it might interest the reader to know that one of the children in this chapter was originally invited to take part in the project because she is a disabled child, with a disabled parent and other disabled relatives. Contrary to our expectations, however, disability was not the main determinant of her reflections on family life. Having a gay parent was another issue that did not merit a mention.

Thinking Points

- Make some notes on what you regard as the essential elements for enabling family life to be sustained when parents are separated. Find out more about how a split family you know manages this, and about what makes doing so a comfortable (or, conversely, a difficult) business. Does existing family law help?

- How might you further your understanding of split family life? What sources of information are available to you? Think about children with whom you have contact, as well as appropriate colleagues and relevant sources of literature.

- What can be done to affirm a child's identity as a member of a coherent family when their family is split? What strategies are needed to ensure that children's family relationships remain positive when parents live apart?

- How can you ensure that you retain a sufficiently broad view of split family life? Can you identify any personal prejudices? For example, are you open to the possibility that relationships may **not** always be worth supporting when a family is split? Take stock of your own ideas about split family life at this point in reading the book, and think about how your views impact on children's lives.

Chapter 6

Family Lives of Hearing Children with Deaf Parents

Sarah Beazley and Michele Moore

Introduction

This chapter arises from several hours that Sarah Beazley spent talking with children whose parents are Deaf.[2] Their thoughts on family life suggest that they consider daily life at home as ordinary and, contrary to the public image of children whose parents are disabled, have no thought of themselves as martyrs. Their accounts do, however, illustrate the ways in which society not only puts up barriers round parents who have impairments but also disables their families in the process (Beazley and Moore, 1995; Corker, 1996; Moore, Beazley and Maelzer, forthcoming; Oliver, 1990, 1996).

The aim of this chapter is to put forward the views Jane, Scott and Huw have of family and home life, focusing particularly upon their experiences as children of Deaf parents. Of course, they talked of family issues beyond hearing impairment, which were of equal if not greater significance for them, and these too are presented. As in all chapters, it has been difficult to extract quotes from the many hours of talking. Each child had plenty to say about their own lives within the family, all of it relevant and revealing.

Scott, aged 15, and Huw, aged 12, are brothers. Scott summarized who is in his family, and then explained which members are hearing impaired:

Scott: Well, there's Huw and Jonathan and mum and Martin.
Interviewer: That's your mother's boyfriend?
Scott: Yeah. It's his (points to Jonathan) real dad, so he's our step-brother.
Interviewer: He's your half-brother.
Scott: Yeah, Half-brother, yeah. We treat him just the same.

Interviewer: What can you describe about your family? What sort of family are you?

---

[2] The word 'deaf' is spelt with a small 'd' when it describes the physical condition of deafness, and with a capital 'D' when it refers to the culture of Deaf people. This distinction is now an accepted convention in literature on sociocultural aspects of deafness. Where community membership is unclear from the context, the 'd/D' form is used.

> *Scott*: Well, my granddad's deaf.
> *Interviewer*: Right.
> *Scott*: That's because he's older he's not . .
> *Interviewer*: Right that's different from your mum.
> *Scott*: Yeah.
> *Interviewer*: What about your dad? Is he deaf?
> *Scott*: Yeah, he's deaf, yeah. Partially deaf, not as deaf as my mum.
> *Interviewer*: Right.
> *Scott*: And my mum's boyfriend is partially deaf.
> *Interviewer*: Right.
> *Scott*: Um, um, my grandma's not. She's, she's OK. Er, my dad lives with my grandma.

Jane is 17, and her family consists of:

> I've got my mum, my dad and my younger brother who's 14. My dad's partially deaf and my mum's deaf. My dad's eyes are bad.

All three were interested in the idea of a book using children's own views of family life and were evidently working hard to understand and explain their situations. Preston (1994) interviewed adults who had Deaf parents, and identified as an underlying commonality their struggle to make sense of the 'socially significant variable' in their upbringing. He also goes on to say that those he met did not consider their own parents 'accountable for whatever difficulties they . . experienced', but considered the source of any problems in childhood to be 'a lack of choices, social oppression . . economic limitations and communication barriers'. The dilemma that emerges is that it appears to be hearing people who make deafness problematic.

Children's Reflections

Are Hearing Children of d/Deaf Parents Burdened with Extra Responsibilities?

There is a widespread, and regrettable, image of children with disabled parents as burdened with roles that the impairment is assumed to prevent their parents from fulfilling (Segal and Simkins, 1993; Aldridge and Becker, 1993a, 1993b). Children in such families are presumed to lose their childhood through the responsibility of extra duties and through not having the usual support from parents. In the process they are expected to be stoic and angelic at all times. The stories of Scott, Huw and Jane do not bear out this impression at all, however. For them, family and home offer a secure base in which they can have fun, get angry or just take things easy. The joys, and trials and tribulations, of family life with disabled parents are revealed to be just as varied and unpredictable as those described by children in any other kind of family explored within this book, and there are many lessons for those supporting children with disabled parents in this observation. Jane, for example, says of her parents:

> We always have a laugh. [You] know you can be dead relaxed [with them].

And about her home:

> You just know, don't you, that home is home. And when you're at work you just feel 'I wish I was at home' [where] you just feel so relaxed.

In comparing her family to that of her best friend, Lisa, Jane is in no doubt that her parents have provided her with positive influences and a clear framework of how to conduct her life:

> I say both families are like very sensible. They know everything, what's right and what's wrong. Like none of them drink or smoke. And I think like they're just dead sensible. They've taught me and Lisa how to grow up. See we went to school with like other people and they was taking things like Es and things like that and me and Lisa turned round and said, 'No way could we do that,' because we knew like, what families we was brought up from.

Far from suffering, the children indicate that there are many short- and long-term advantages of family life with d/Deaf parents. This emerged as the first issue in Sarah's conversation with Scott and Huw:

> *Interviewer*: So imagine if you were talking to someone who hadn't met you before, what would it be like to live in your family?
> *Scott*: It's a bit different because like we get away with little things because mum can't hear us.
> *Interviewer*: What sort of things?
> *Scott*: Just like if we shout loud and we can have the TV a bit louder than everybody else. [We] just get away with things like that. So when friends come they always say, 'How come you're allowed to shout so loud? We're not at our house.' And you just say, 'Because she can't hear us so it's all right.'

> *Interviewer* [*to Huw*]: What sort of things do you get away with?
> *Huw*: Erm, say mum told me off or something I can back chat her sometimes and she can't hear me.

They both had a giggle as they talked about such incidents. On the other hand, throughout the conversation they also talked frequently of the support they get from their parents, for example:

Interviewer: If either of you feel upset, who do you talk to?
Scott and Huw: Mum.
Interviewer: She's the one you find it easiest to talk to?
Scott and Huw: Yeah.

and:

Scott: Martin usually helps us with our homework.

And if they did something wrong, it was, as Scott said, 'Well, just like normal families,' with the usual reprimands which they accepted as part of family life. They gave no hint that they were more, or indeed less, circumspect about their behaviour at home than any other child their age.

Jane talks of a possible long-term benefit of being the hearing child of Deaf parents. She shows a great interest and pride in her mother's first language, British Sign Language (BSL) and has developed sufficient skill to enjoy using it at an informal level. She may even turn to a career in interpreting:

Jane: I love going out with my mum. People try to talk to her and communicate and I'll just step in and say, 'Look she said this and that.' I like signing for her as well. Telling her what they're saying. Like the other night, she teaches at the [local] primary, and it was someone's 18th birthday and we went for a drink afterwards and because they were all hearing they was all talking and I was signing. So I like doing that.
Interviewer: Would you like to become an interpreter?
Jane: Yeah, I'm hoping to. I knew [a friend's] mum was Deaf and I said to her, I said, 'Do you enjoy signing?' She says, 'Oh, yeah,' she says, 'I'm hoping to interpret for my mum's wedding.' She's getting married in three weeks. I thought 'I'd love to do that' because she's [going to] be so proud . . . like you'd be so proud of your mum and [she'd] be proud of you.

The different way of communicating, then, was not seen as an encumbrance, but, on the contrary, a pleasure and an achievement. Given that there is no evidence that these three children felt burdened with extra responsibilities, it is useful to see how the children perceived differences between their family lives and those of peers with non-disabled parents.

Communication in the Home

All three children talked throughout the interviews about ways of communicating within their family context and the impact these had upon family life. Whilst at least one parent in both families was a sign language user, BSL was not the main language of either home. The children described a variety of strategies for establishing effective communication with their parents:

> *Scott*: We communicate with just lip-reading.
> *Interviewer*: So neither of you use [the sign language you've learnt]?
> *Scott*: Well, I do, just a little bit. You know for sometimes if [my mum] doesn't understand my lip-reading or if I talk too fast . . it's just the common signs.
> *Huw*: I just talk to my mum. I'm just used to it now. [She] just lip-reads me. I know some of the common signs, signing the alphabet and 'thank you' and things like that. But I never use them.

> *Jane*: [My mum] can hear if you shout at her and things. I don't really sign to her even though I do know sign language. I don't sign to her. I talk to her. My mum knows what I'm saying because she can lip-read me all the time. But my dad, you have to shout when you're speaking.

Both of the mothers, the main sign language users in each home, were brought up to use spoken language at a time when BSL was given little credibility and there was great emphasis placed upon the value of speech (Gregory and Hartley, 1991). Jane makes reference to the detrimental impact this has had upon everyday family life for herself, her mother and her gran:

> My mum went to a deaf school in Southfield and the teachers told my gran never to sign to her, always to talk her. But nowadays I think it's easier for her to sign to her but she doesn't know it now because she's been taught to speak to her ever since she's grown up . . . She sits there and she'll say it like ten times if she has to . . . if she comes here when my mum's got some friends here . . my gran's wondering what they're saying. Now if she could sign, she could join in as well . . . but my gran will sit there reading a magazine. I'm thinking, 'Why don't you join in, Gran?'

Today, Deaf people are seeking greater recognition for sign language (Corker, 1993; Kenyon, 1994); the oppressive insistence on d/Deaf people to use speech is easing and alternative bilingual approaches are being explored (Bouvet, 1990; Gregory, Wells and Smith, 1996). Scott talks about the direct impact this has had upon his family:

> Mum's going to bring [Jonathan] up signing . . . mum regrets that she never brought us up on sign language and speaking.

Scott and Huw also explained some of the practical problems that they faced at home with regard to communication and the solutions that had been found:

> *Scott*: We have to bang on the floor like if we want her for something. Like other people just shout at their mum, 'Mum,' we'd have to like bang on the floor like, er, making vibration.

Interviewer: And does that work OK?
Scott: Yeah, mostly, unless she's upstairs. We have to go upstairs to tell her.

Interviewer: What happens in your home about the phone and door?
Scott: The door bell flashes. Just downstairs though. Same with the phone. The phone flashes when it rings. Mostly we just answer it anyway because we rush to the phone anyway because it's usually one of our friends anyway!

Scott: And if there's someone at the door like we have to go and, we have to explain to the person and say like she's deaf and everything, isn't it?
Interviewer: How does that make you feel?
Scott: I don't know, just got used to it.
Interviewer: You're used to it. What about you?
Huw: I'm used to it. And it's the same when the telephone rings and I have to explain things for mum. I'm just used to it now . . . sometimes, like if we go to some other houses we get a bit jealous because they can just shout, 'Mum, Mum.' We can't do that so . . but it's . . we don't mind, do we? Just get used to it . . . they always shout from upstairs [or] downstairs if they want their tea or if the phone's ringing or [shout] 'Somebody's at the door, Mum.'

Although children with d/Deaf parents evolve measures which may seem different to those of their friends with hearing parents, these become a part of everyday family life which they become 'just used to'. These strategies enable the family to function effectively and are not seen as of much concern for Scott and Huw.

Jane, too, makes little mention of the day-to-day communication strategies within her family. She explained how her dad tries to ensure everyone is included in the conversation:

My dad will sign as he's talking to me and [my brother] so [my mum] knows what he's said to us.

The only other mention of communication tactics came when commenting on her own options if she wanted to draw her mother's attention to something:

[My mum] can't see like properly from, you know, far distance so I have to sign.

There are times when the well-established ways of communicating do break down and Scott and Huw brought up a couple of examples where this happens:

Scott: Sometimes [mum] gets frustrated because we talk too fast or we cover our mouths or something and she's always saying, 'Uncover your mouth because I can't tell what you're saying.'

and:

> *Scott*: Sometimes we're talking, say if we're going out somewhere we shout, 'We're going out now,' and we come back and she'll say, 'Where have you been?'
> *Huw*: We said we told her, but she never heard.
> *Scott*: She never heard, so we get told off.

On the whole, though, the communication system between the family members allows for the smooth running of daily life and as such is not an issue of great consequence to the children. However, any family communication is not simply dependent upon the means of exchanging messages and views, but also upon the motivation to relate to others at home. When this seems uncertain, a problem may be perceived. Jane is very concerned about her 14-year-old brother, Peter, who is rebelling against her parents and exploiting their need to use a different channel of communication:

> Well, he's not good at signing. He gets impatient and mum can't understand what he's saying because he doesn't talk with his mouth, he talks with his tongue like that [*demonstrates*]. Then she gets angry because he's getting impatient because she doesn't know what he's said. Weird.

and:

> *Jane*: I think he likes to take advantage of my mum and dad because of them being deaf and dad's partially deaf and well, he's not quite blind anymore, he's been able to get his sight back now, but it's very often [Peter] takes advantage because he knows that he can get away with it and he's not pressurized.
> *Interviewer*: And what do your mum and dad say to him?
> *Jane*: Nothing because they can't hear him. That's what I'm trying to say, yeah.
> *Interviewer*: So it's extra pressure on you then?
> *Jane*: Yeah. My dad hears it sometimes because he'll say, 'Will you watch your mouth?'

It is clearly painful for Jane to observe her brother's behaviour towards their parents and to feel the negative vibes of his backchat. Jane's view of family life is greatly influenced by her brother's current behaviour and her anxieties about the effect this is having on her parents too:

> *Jane*: I feel like I need to help them a bit . . .
> *Interviewer*: So how do you see the future?
> *Jane*: Can't predict it. I can see Peter growing out of this behaviour at 18. So we've still got another few years ahead of us.

The children's comments illustrate that, in their families, the **process** of communication is as unpredictable over time as in any other family context and for periods can disturb the balance of things. However, the comments of all three children suggest that, although the communication **mode** may be different within their family situations, it is not this that disrupts family functioning in any way. It is important to recognize that any extra responsibilities Jane does feel, do not arise because her parents have impaired hearing, but stem from the lack of support that is available to them.

We would now like to consider what the children had to say about the wider circumstances in which their families function and discuss the communication and attitudinal barriers they encounter and which impact upon all three of them.

Disabling Barriers

The experience of disability stems from environmental and attitudinal barriers which people with impairments have to confront on a daily basis (Corker, 1996; Keith, 1994; Morris, 1991, 1993; Oliver, 1990, 1996). Within a family, where attitudes and environmental barriers are minimized, hearing children and their d/Deaf parents do not experience disablement. All of the children realized this. Unfortunately, they were all able to illustrate how other people outside the family contribute to the oppression of their parents and themselves through prejudice and disabling attitudes. Two particularly compelling examples reveal ignorance and sheer lack of thought on the part of professionals where, at planned meetings, they had not taken responsibility to check that the communication context was one where the parent would get equal access to information without resorting to dependency upon the child. Jane is attempting to explain how it feels to be in that position but it is not easy, given her own sense of responsibility for ensuring her mother is informed, weighed against the power relations involved at such a meeting. She describes a parents' evening:

> *Interviewer*: So your teacher had to say to you how you'd done and you had to sign that to your mum?
> *Jane*: Yeah.
> *Interviewer*: Wasn't that uncomfortable?
> *Jane*: Well, it was funny because my mum just sits there . . . and I'm thinking, 'Mum I'm supposed to have done bad,' or you know something but she's like, 'Yeah' like dead proud. It's like I say, 'Oh, I didn't do well in my exam,' she says, 'Yeah, but I'm still happy.'
> *Interviewer*: And how did the teachers deal with the situation?
> *Jane*: Well, some of them talked to her you know afterwards. Some of them. And she said that she liked some of them, the ones that could talk to her. But some of them just ignored her. And she don't like that.

Interviewer: How did you feel?
Jane: I just felt, 'Well thank you . . I used to like you,' you know what I mean. It's weird how you feel in a position like that.

Being expected to interpret or even to speak on behalf of your parents often brings about a switch in the social roles of the parent and child which can be a strain on the child and demeaning for the parent. Of course, this problem is not brought about because parents are hearing impaired, but because hearing people hold disabling attitudes about their own responsibilities for easy and effective communication with d/Deaf people. Scott explains a similar situation when he accompanied his mum to take his younger brother to the speech and language therapist, and found he was having to help his mother put forward alternative views:

> But she's saying [Jonathan's late emerging speech] is because mum's deaf and he doesn't know what words sound like. And we say, 'No, because we speak normal.'

Scott has to challenge the disabling stereotypical image which the therapist holds about d/Deaf people and communication. At 15, he realizes that his family is being oppressed less by hearing impairment than by the short-comings of others in responding to difference.

Thus, children with d/Deaf parents are regularly placed in uncomfortable or unfair situations which they may become more prepared for over time but which can still prove damaging. In addition, such encounters may lead to some disparities between the views they hold of their parents and those held of them by society at large. The children also become acutely aware of common prejudices against people with impairments. They recounted several incidents which show how reactions to their family as different can have social and economic effects which disable the family as a whole and also each individual member. Huw speaks here of acting as spontaneous communicator between their mother and others in town:

> Sometimes we're shopping or something like that, erm, and they say something to my mum and she just didn't quite get what they said and so we have to explain through what they said. But it doesn't bother me because I'm just helping my mum.

His brother Scott expects to deal with other people's disabling behaviour on a regular basis:

> Sometimes, like in the supermarket . . . like somebody comes up to [my mum] and says, 'Excuse me,' she doesn't move sometimes be-cause she can't hear them. So the woman gets a bit, or the man, gets a bit aggro. So I have to say [to mum] 'Excuse, someone's coming past' like. So they go past and they sometimes look.

Scott, Huw and Jane are all also aware of the repercussions of other restrictions placed on their parents, ones which reduce opportunities for d/Deaf people to play full roles in the majority culture due to educational, employment and social barriers. They talk about their parents' limited access to the school curriculum:

> *Scott*: At school [mum] like only got learnt some things.
> *Interviewer*: So she didn't get a full chance to learn everything.
> *Scott*: Yeah.
> *Huw*: No.
> *Scott*: But Martin did because he's only partially deaf, so he did learn everything, so he helps us more.

They also talk about the separation from family experienced by their parents due to attending segregated residential schools:

> *Scott*: Because like when she went to a boarding school, a deaf school. She went to Newfield and so then met my dad . . . that's why we're live here and not in Wales.

Jane feels her family have been disabled financially because her mother's employment prospects have been limited and understands how this could have a direct impact upon her own career choices:

> *Jane*: It's difficult because [cousins going to university] they've got quite a lot of money and we, this family, haven't you see, because my mum's brothers are hearing and that, so . . [*breaks off*]
> *Interviewer*: Do you think that's made a difference then?
> *Jane*: Yeah. I think it has.

Jane also notes that her mother's circle of friends, established through school, the Deaf Club and work, are not close by:

> I think she's a bit jealous because my friend's always here and she doesn't have friends coming round because they live so far away. She just makes friends that are so far away. I mean her best friend lives in Southbrook. The other couple that she gets on with, she doesn't see often. They live in Wardlington.

Huw knows that the wider community discriminates against his parents and himself through perpetuating environmental barriers:

> *Huw*: When I go out to play or something like that and Martin's not in I can't ring up home and say that I'm going to be back home late because my mum can't answer the phone. So that's a problem as well.

Interviewer: Unless you've got a Minicom.
Huw: Yeah, but they don't have them in public phoneboxes.

This immediately limits Huw's choices on a day-to-day level and adds to his already keenly developing sense of society's lack of justice.

Similarly, the children discern that the adult world is not only unfair but that it prejudges others. As society often portrays children of people with impairments as martyrs, so it perpetuates images of disabled people of anything from pitiable burdens to objects of fear (Barnes, 1992). Jane recalls a situation which highlights the disabling effects such images can have on family life:

Jane: There is one thing that's quite hard to find out is why me dad's family are so far apart from me mum. They never communicate with her.
Interviewer: And you've no idea why that is.
Jane: No. I think its because they're scared . . [*breaks off*]
Interviewer: Because she's deaf?
Jane: Mmm.
Interviewer: They just don't know how to . .
Jane: . . Communicate with her. And they just totally ignore her when they're sat in this room. I find it difficult to say to them, 'Why won't you communicate with my mum? It's not so hard.'

Scott has a real dilemma with society's lack of acceptance of his mother, based upon the dissonance between his knowledge of her and the prejudicial behaviour that he has observed. He verbalizes his confusion at several points by raising the image of her as not deaf:

Scott: Well about a couple of years ago, they were talking, my nanna and taid [Granddad], in Wales, about having something, an operation on my mum. Something about implants or something in her ear.
Interviewer: Yeah, that's right, called a cochlear implant.
Scott: Yeah, something that they pay for to see if she could speak better but I don't know what happened. I suppose mum didn't want to because she's got used to it. I mean if she did have this she could hear how she spoke and it'd be funny because she doesn't, she, she, she knows that she can't hear our own voices, she doesn't know how we speak, properly, so I suppose it's a bit hard that for her.

In response to a question about what they would say to others in their circumstances, Huw answered first, with Scott again showing some reservations:

Huw: I'd say, don't let it get in the way and just . .
Scott: Don't let it bother you.

> *Huw*: Don't let it bother you and . .
> *Interviewer*: That's good advice. Is that how you feel about it?
> *Scott*: Well, we can't stop her being deaf so we have to . .
> *Huw*: We just get on with it.

and later, at the very end of our conversation:

> *Interviewer*: Right, I think we're nearly there. So any more things you
> feel you want to say . . . no?
> *Scott*: . . Obviously we wish she wasn't deaf. We know it's there like.
> We wish she were hearing but because it would probably hurt her
> feelings but . . it's just like we have got used to it, haven't we? Some-
> times I think, it sounds a bit horrible, but just 'Why me?' because other
> people are not. But . . . like we say, we've just got used to it. So we're
> just OK. Everybody knows. So it's just normal really. Except that . .
> *Huw*: You just get on.
> *Interviewer*: Yeah, you just get on with your life.
> *Scott*: Yeah.

In terms of his day-to-day life, Scott's family life is ordinary to him and it is his mother to whom he turns if he is in any difficulty. Yet he knows that his family is set apart because she is Deaf and he feels the associated social stigma. Children, by virtue of their status in society, generally understand what it feels like to be without influence (Van der Klift and Kunc, 1994) and Scott has to view his mother as disregarded and powerless in a similar way. In addition, as Preston (1994) points out, hearing children of deaf parents can face uncer-tainty about their cultural identity. They know that hearing people make deaf-ness problematic but they themselves are physically hearing; do they consider themselves as culturally Deaf, or Hearing, or as straddling the two in some way?

Discrimination against children whose parents are d/Deaf arises through educational and attitudinal barriers erected by society, institutions and indi-viduals over time. Such barriers cause social as well as financial restrictions and influence any child with disabled parents. Fortunately, Scott and the other two children have informal support networks around them for manag-ing their everyday life, which include the family and also reaching beyond to the extended family and friends. The next section considers this tremendous resource that all three children identified within their lives.

Support Networks Beyond the Immediate Family

Family, friends and the Deaf community all provide a wide range of support for Scott, Huw and Jane. They help in careers decisions:

Jane: Margaret that my mum used to work with . . I do get her to look at my letters and transfer them like into good English. And it has helped me get interviews and things like that.

Jane: [My gran] helps me a bit . . . me cousins, they're been so good. Like Liz, she's gone to, is it Hull University or something? So she knows quite a bit about their careers. And she's trying to encourage me to do something a bit more higher.

Jane: I like talking to people like [at the Deaf Club] and finding out, you know, what they've been doing all week and like there's a lot of the [Deaf people] now, you know, that teach sign language and I keep thinking, 'Where's it all come from?' You know, it's just come out of the blue, so sudden. I'm thinking, 'I'd like to do that I think.'

People beyond the immediate family help children on practical matters:

Jane: My neighbour's quite good because he gives me lifts every-where normally.

and by just listening:

Jane: I had a good chat to [gran] last week on the phone and she, she's like telling me a few things that I was a bit iffy about.

Jane: Sometimes I ring [Lisa] up and say, 'Oh, so and so has upset me at work and I've had enough.'

Jane: Margaret . . . 20 years ago she used to work with my mum at the town hall, so she knew what me mum was like when she was younger. And I do go in work sometimes and she goes, 'Sit down, just tell me.' And I tell her and she gives it, 'You're just going to have to put up with it because you're only young.'

Huw: I could talk to my grandma.
Scott: It's not a lot. If it is a problem more to that side of the family we do talk to her. If it's right at this side of the family we talk to our mum.

Interviewer: What about when you met some of the other children with deaf parents, did that help?
Scott: Yeah, we could talk to each other about what it was like.
Huw: Yeah, just felt a bit better because we know other people have got the same problems and things like that.

Friends play broader roles as well, and Huw talks about the closeness between his family and that of his best friend:

> *Huw*: [My best friend] lives at the bottom of the street who plays for the same football team, same age as me, called Tom. His dad is the manager of Townsend football team and so Martin's always talking with [Tom's dad] and going down there and talking a lot and my mum's good friends with Lynn, because . .
>
> *Scott*: Because she's taking sign language courses and also she signs a lot with mum.

Communication here between the families is easy and the support reaches more widely than just to Huw. Other friends also adapt to the situation quickly with barriers soon broken down:

> *Scott*: My old friends from primary school they used to get on well with my mum. But David I can tell he's still a bit shy with speaking to her. When he first come, everybody's, when they first come they don't say much because they don't know what's going to happen. But he's getting used to it.
>
> *Interviewer*: So how do you feel with that, with your friends being a bit unsure about talking to your mum?
>
> *Scott*: Just say, 'It's OK if you get stuck talking to her, just ask me and I'll tell her what you're saying or tell you what she's saying to you.'
>
> *Interviewer*: Yeah.
>
> *Scott*: So it's, it's OK. I just tell them to be comfortable, its just like normal but she's deaf. That's all. We just have to when we make new friends just have to tell them that like, 'Our mum's deaf and sometimes if you want to speak to her just tell me and I'll tell her' or 'if you want to try and speak, yeah'. 'And she understands what everybody else says mostly by lip-reading.'

It is telling to note that professionals, such as social workers or teachers do not figure in these accounts of who offers support to children with deaf parents.

As other chapter writers in this book have found, informal networks play an important role in the family and home lives of the children we met, and the support of others outside the immediate family adds to a child's sense of security and belonging. Such a network of familiar people to talk to is helpful when there are issues facing the children that perhaps cannot so easily be discussed with parents or siblings. Many other topics that the children interviewed for this chapter discussed also highlighted similarities between their lives and those of their peers in the wide variety of family situations covered in this book.

Other Family Issues

Jane, Scott and Huw all talked about other family issues apart from relating directly to having Deaf parents. They talked of playing music, computers, bike rides, football, cars, learning to drive, life with a baby brother, family weddings, wanting the home decorated, and of other ordinary things. There were recurring themes in both interviews which merit discussion because they challenge stereotypical notions about the preoccupations of children whose parents are disabled.

Scott and Huw come back often in their accounts to their experience of life in a split family:

Scott: Dad plays for the Deaf football team . . well he used to play for them . . but they're not very much . . friends now because . . I don't know . .
Interviewer: Not so comfortable.
Scott: No. Like my mum and my real dad they don't . . they don't speak to each other now.
Interviewer: How does that make you feel?
Scott: I wish they did. Mum would like to get to know him again, not to get to know him again, but like to make friends with him, but my dad's a bit stubborn.

Huw: We don't go [to the Deaf Club] as much as we used to because . .
Interviewer: Because?
Huw: Um, my dad goes a lot. He goes . . Because they've split up we don't go as much now.
Scott: He's club secretary so . .
Interviewer: It's awkward to go.
Scott: Yeah. If we do go, it's either with my dad alone or with my mum alone. Not both together. But if it does happen together then it's just a bit awkward, it's just . . my dad's on one side and mum on the other and you don't know which to go to.

Scott: She don't come here, grandma.
Huw: She used to come like a lot.
Interviewer: Oh, why doesn't she visit?
Scott: It's just my dad. He's never been here since they broke up.
Interviewer: So you grandma thinks your dad wouldn't like it, is that it?
Scott: Yes.
Interviewer: So you'd like in the future for you all to be able to get together whenever you want.
Scott: Know each other, yeah. See if it's a wedding, my wedding or something, I'd like everybody to come together, talk to each other. Not like one side of my family that's one side and that's one side. Just mix and everything.

The two children see their dad regularly and enjoy doing a range of activities with him. They also have strong relationships with their mother and their step-father. As discussed in Chapter 5, they have the benefits of three parents. They no longer have stresses associated with parents splitting up, which Scott remembers as being 'hard for me'. They do express their wish that the adults got on better, but it is clear from all the children's reflections in this book, that parents rarely manage to make children's experiences of home and family life perfect.

For Jane, one of her main worries is her teenage brother. Concerns about him surfaced early in her interview:

> To be honest it's like quite tense [in my family] because you've got one of their children who is always bad and is always lying to them and that's my brother but he's, he's .. very hard to live with because ... he's always had his own way and now he's getting older he's not getting his way as much and it's a bit of a .. he's very .. moody all the time. So I've got to try and help [my parents]. We're just living through it day by day. It's really hard. Really hard. Because I know that they've not got .. the .. [*long pause*] .. can't think of the word .. they've not got enough courage to shout at him or, not smack him, but you know give him a real good telling off. So that's how he knows that he can get away with it.

A lack of family support services has led Jane to believe that **she** is responsible for enabling family life:

> *Jane*: I keep saying that I'm going to move out, I'm going to move out when I get a pay rise next June, but .. I don't think I could do it on my own. I know I'd miss it too much here.
> *Interviewer*: [Your parents] would manage without you?
> *Jane*: My mum wouldn't. She wouldn't know how to. She always says, 'Oh, you're not leaving, you're not leaving.'
> *Interviewer*: How do you feel about that?
> *Jane*: Something inside's telling me that I've got to go even though .. I don't want to let my mum down.

We would argue that it is a indictment upon our society if children are compelled to support their parents with impairment-related daily assistance. There is provision within the Independent Living Fund for people with impairments to have a full assessment of their needs and a requirement for needs identified to be met (Morris, 1993). Somewhere along the line, children like Jane, and their disabled parents, are being profoundly let down by a lack of support for their families.

All three children have many parts to their lives within their families as is clearly illustrated here. They presented those parts which absorbed them in ways which reflect their own concerns at the time and also their response to what they considered Sarah might be expecting of them. The partial nature of the children's reflections is taken up again in the concluding chapter of this book.

Family Life with Deaf Parents: Hearing Children's Perspectives

The accounts Jane and Scott and Huw gave of family life resembled each other in a number of ways. They all viewed home and family as a secure and central part of their own lives but also showed that they were able to be reflexive about family life, trying to make sense of the actions and roles of all those involved and to take their own unfolding position on happenings: past, present and future.

All three children also talked of the practical issues involved in having hearing and Deaf members in their families, relating particularly to communication strategies used. They also demonstrated a sharp awareness of the prejudices against d/Deaf people and gave examples of how others, through ignorance, thoughtlessness or even fear, made life more difficult for their parents, themselves and the whole family.

There were differences too in their stories. Jane, at 17, was starting to look more closely at her own rapidly approaching adult life and the choices that she would have to make for herself which might mean moving away from home. This prospect was one she was finding hard to face. Also emerging from Jane's conversation was her pride in her mother as a Deaf person and her own increasing contact with the Deaf Community. She recognizes and enjoys Deaf culture and speaks with enjoyment about sign language.

Scott and Huw still have their sights in childhood, with home, school work, sport and friends the main focus for them. Their experience as part of a split family is as much a significant feature in their view of family life as their parents' hearing impairment. Certainly, Scott is expressing some confusion in his feelings about his mother's deafness and he feels others' lack of acceptance of difference deeply. Huw, who is younger and also has a best friend whose family have worked to avoid communication, attitudinal and other barriers, seems less troubled by the issues unsettling Scott. Thus, once again, we can see that it is a lack of support which disables children whose parents are deaf, not hearing impairment *per se*.

Quite obviously, this chapter does not set out to portray the essence of children's views of family life with d/Deaf parents, and indeed it would be dangerous to attempt any such generalization. Rather, the stories presented here are a reminder of the range of issues that might face any child whose parents are disabled and the different weighting that the child might attach to each.

Methodological Issues

In addition to the wider range of methodological issues relating to researching children's views that have been discussed elsewhere in this book, there a number that relate specifically to these interviews.

The first we wish to mention is that the children Sarah met were all hearing children of Deaf parents. The stories of d/Deaf children of d/Deaf parents would have added another dimension to the chapter. The Deaf community feel that the family with all d/Deaf members has a unique and important perspective (Robinson, 1995) which reflects the far-reaching effects of belonging to a linguistic and cultural minority. We agree with this point, but it does not in any way lessen the value of the contribution given by the three children who did participate in this project.

The second issue relates to the presence of the parents at the interviews. Both meetings took place at the children's homes with mothers there at each and Jane's father was also present whilst she was talking. At the children's request, the interviews were not conducted in sign language but in spoken language only. Although their parents were in the same room, they were involved in other activities such as watching television or preparing food and hence could neither hear nor lip-read the conversation. Sarah was not entirely at ease about this situation herself as she felt the children needed privacy in order to be able to say what they wished. However, the children all seemed comfortable with this arrangement and talked quite freely throughout. Also, as time progressed, it became evident that none of the parents intended to participate in any way and were used to letting the children talk uninterrupted at the other end of the room.

A third issue became visible as Jane spoke with some strength of feeling about some of the issues facing her despite having explained that if she was upset 'I generally keep it to myself' and that she was 'Quite quiet. A bit shy really about new people.' She spoke about some very personal concerns and would like to have talked some more. Towards the end of the meeting, she said, 'Thanks for helping me bring it out,' and her eyes were tearful. Clearly she was finding herself talking about matters close to her heart and should, perhaps, have been encouraged to consider ways forward and to identify people who could help her to pursue some of the issues she was raising. This exposes one of the many dilemmas researchers face when they interview children in difficult situations, and we return to these in the concluding chapter.

These interviews give a brief insight in to the preoccupations of hearing children whose parents are deaf. Not all children in this situation will share all, or perhaps any, of these concerns. The reflections are important, however, because they prompt us to focus less on problems assumed to be associated with impairment, and more on the impact that disabling attitudes and environmental barriers have on children's lives (Beazley and Moore, 1995; Oliver, 1996).

Thinking Points

- If you were meeting a d/Deaf parent for the first time, consider how you would ensure that they had equal access to information without using their child to act as a go-between in communication.

- Note some of the images portraying adults with impairments in the media. In what ways to these images enable or, conversely, disable children whose parent(s) have impairment?

- In what ways could children who have a disabled parent be helped to explore experiences of disabling prejudice?

- Think of any particular impairment. List the barriers a child could face if a parent had this impairment. Think about difficulties in different aspects of everyday family and home life. For each potential problem you have envisaged, identify at least one strategy for dismantling it.

- How can children whose parents are disabled be supported in raising awareness about their family situation with their peers? Draw up a 10-point plan for developing such an awareness-raising project.

- What are the implications for children if negative images of disabled parents prevail? Can you identify any ways in which your own preconceptions have been challenged by what Jane, or Huw or Scott, have had to say?

Chapter 7

Asian Family Life

Usha Rout, Judith Sixsmith and Michele Moore

Introduction

Two children of Asian parents living in Britain are the focus of this chapter. As Priestley (1995) points out, there is, of course, 'much ambiguity in the definition of being Asian'. Both children whose experiences are recounted here, are second-generation British Asian children of immigrant first-generation Asian parents. As in all the chapters of this book, it is very important to recognize that the chapter is based on two children's subjective reflections on family life, and no commonality is claimed with reference to any other children living in Britain with Asian connections.

It is worth pointing this out early in the chapter as inappropriate stereotypical images of Asian children as a homogenous group often prevail in British culture. Just as British society as a whole is pluralistic, Asian communities have differences as well as similarities in cultural activities, beliefs, language, social class, lifestyles, their country of origin, and many other factors, between them. It is important that the children who took part in this project are not viewed as members of a single Asian community, disregarding some of the distinct differences. Although there may exist unity and solidarity among culturally diverse and ethnically distinctive groups it is not possible to make any broad generalizations about them (Priestly, 1995). This chapter is simply concerned with uncovering two children's understanding of their personal experiences as members of Asian families living within a British context. There is no motivation to present this material as representative of all Asian children's experiences. As with interview material presented throughout the book, the data is intended to be illustrative and thought provoking.

There has been some research into the experience of Asian family life in Britain (Anwar, 1981; Kitwood, 1983; Westwood and Bhachu, 1988), including the dilemmas of second-generation young people living in Britain compared to their first-generation parents (Stopes-Roe and Cochrane, 1990), and the challenge of coping with two cultures (Wade and Souter, 1992). But few studies have given young Asian children the opportunity to speak freely and openly about their own experiences of home and family life in depth. This chapter aims to do just this by giving two young Asian children an opportunity to speak about their experiences and concerns. This aim is more easily stated than achieved.

As is apparent throughout this book, children need to be helped and encouraged to speak up about their experiences. With specific reference to this chapter, there can be difficulty in revealing the cultural realities in which Asian children are immersed. The social-cultural background of the researcher can play an important part in setting the research agenda, guiding the interviews and managing the relationship between interviewer and interviewee. Care needs to be taken, particularly in work with culturally diverse families, so that the cultural integrity of the families studied remains as intact as possible. Attention to the 'cultural landscape' with which children are familiar, and also to different cultural realities is important in a study of Asian children's experiences of family life (Dilworth-Anderson *et al.*, 1993). It would be very easy for a poorly informed interviewing style to reduce children's confidence for expressing their own cultural norms, beliefs, attitudes and behaviours. For this reason, we were glad to have Usha Rout as a member of our research team, who, as an Asian woman living in Britain, could take on the task of interviewing Asian children from a relatively aware 'insider' perspective. By being appreciative of relevant cultural issues, because she originates from an Asian background and is herself raising children in Britain, Usha hoped that the children would feel able to open up and talk freely about their family experiences.

Before proceeding with the interviews which are central to this chapter, Usha undertook pilot interviews with two Asian girls, aged 5- and 11-years-old, from different social backgrounds. Both were known to her previously through Asian social gatherings. These interviews provided an opportunity to prepare for the task of interviewing two Asian children for the main study: Imran, a Muslim boy aged 11; and Meena, a Hindu girl aged 15.

Children's Reflections

Imran

Imran was an independent, bright and happy child known to Usha through family social gatherings. At the time of the interview, Imran was 11 years old. He lived with his parents, a younger sister, Zarina aged 10 and a brother, Naman aged 7. The family lived in a large detached house in an affluent area. His father was a Consultant Physician in a local hospital and owned a private nursing home as well as some properties for rental. Imran's mother did not work outside of the home and spent much of her time caring for Zarina who has a chronic lung disorder. At the time of interview, Zarina was awaiting a lung transplant and she and her mother had to spend a great deal of her time in hospital. Imran and his brother, Naman, usually stayed at home on their own when this happened. Imran's father was busy most of the time at work and looking after his business.

The family belonged to a small Muslim religious community, and Imran said that he mainly socialized with children of the same religious background. This contact with his family's cultural background helped to compensate for the fact that none of Imran's relatives lived in England. His maternal grandparents were deceased and his father's mother lived in India. Several of his cousins lived in different parts of the world, which he was pleased about because it provided him with opportunities for travel:

> I like a big family. You can go to them. They live in different countries and you can visit them. Like I'm going this year to visit my cousin in Africa. His father is a bank manager and his mum is an artist. They come to visit us about once every two years.

As Imran explained above, his family is not confined to Britain. On the contrary, many close family members lived in other countries which enabled him to enjoy the benefits of experiencing life in different cultures and to see himself as part of a global family network with its own sense of togetherness which cuts across geographical boundaries.

In terms of his immediate nuclear family, Imran was very much aware of their status within the Muslim community as well as within the English community. He described his family background as privileged:

> I have a very good family, healthy family, wealthy, you know.

This, he felt, was evidenced by their large family home and he was proud of this. The family's back garden was very large and extended to the nearby woods, which provided opportunity for Imran and his friends to play different games which he freely enjoyed:

> I like a good home, a very big home like a mansion. I like it to be big. I don't like it to be like Justin Taylor, like joint houses, you know. I like it to be as a mansion . . it's got a radio that, you know, you can listen to music. You've got television, you can watch television, you've got computer, you've got satellite, you know like SKY, all the SKY channels. You've got a walkman you can listen to music and . . I like it to have a big garden to play in, and have slides and swings. I like it to have bushes, you know . . . I like getting the fruit out of the trees to eat. I like going to the forest to play with my friends and that.

Due to his father's heavy work commitments and his mother's frequent visits to the hospital, Imran had gained a degree of independence and spent a lot of his time playing with his brother and friends. Imran and his friends were of the same religious community and often played together at weekends when their parents socialized, chatting and eating meals together. These contacts promote the maintenance of the family's preferred culture:

Normally on Saturdays we go to our friends' house. They are our family friends like Uncle Hanif who lives nearer to my house. They have three children like us. They normally come to our house on Fridays. We also go to Uncle Rashid's house who lives in Bainbridge. We have dinner there.

It emerged that Imran's everyday life outside of the school context was very firmly grounded within the local Asian community which he felt was reflected in his own family values, beliefs and attitudes. When comparing his own family to that of his best friend, Imran felt they were very similar:

We go to each other's houses, they have the same number of children, like for example Dr Amad has three children the same like us and you don't get bored because they have the same computer, they like the same sports as us and they like the same TV programmes.

Expectations of children's behaviour were very similar between Imran's best friend's family and his own, and he seemed to gain a sense of security from this. Yet he was also able to see differences between himself and his best friend, based mainly on personal preferences:

Rasheed doesn't like going to parties like I do . . . and he just likes staying at home . . and he likes board games more than sporty games. I don't like board games that much.

When Imran's father was available, mainly during holidays, he and Imran enjoyed shared activities:

My dad takes me to lots of places in the holidays and lets me go like to the park or tennis courts . . we play each other at golf, we play tennis together . . we go to the museum together to learn about the dinosaurs when they were born and we go and we watch TV together, like we watched the football you know, like yesterday. We watched the football yesterday, we watch cricket together. Like, we went to Old Trafford to see West Indies against England in 1990.

Imran valued time together with his dad, particularly when he accompanied his father to work. He loved to do this as he gained insight into his father's working life and also saw the possibilities for his own career in medicine:

Imran: We go to hospital together, like I see what my dad's doing in hospital . . when I grow up I would like to be a doctor like my dad, do medicine, like be a consultant.
Interviewer: Do medicine?
Imran: Yeah, and I like to, you know, go in a hospital like my dad

here in Clare Hospital in Rodmell. I'd like to own, like [a famous] hospital . . you know [like] Great Ormond Street Hospital, one of them hospitals.

Imran was impressed by his father's work and looked to his father as an important role model for this own future. On the other hand, he also enjoyed doing things together with his mother:

> *Interviewer*: What kind of things do you usually do together with your mother?
> *Imran*: We go shopping together, we go to people's houses together. We do gardening together We go for a walk, we tidy-up the home together . . play in the back garden . . cricket.

As his sister was seriously ill, Imran's relationship with her centred around playing board games when she felt able, and he occasionally took some responsibility for looking after her:

> *Interviewer*: What kinds of things do you usually do together with your sister?
> *Imran*: Well, we don't do that much, because she is mostly in hospital but when we are together we go to town. She can't walk. So I sometimes push her [in a wheelchair]. We play board games like snakes and ladders, ludo, chess.

In times of need and distress, Imran felt most comfortable turning to his sister for support. This is perhaps due to the small age gap between his sister and himself, in comparison to the existence of a generation gap between Imran and his parents which sometimes led to conflict:

> *Interviewer*: Who do you talk to when you are upset?
> *Imran*: Oh well it depends. There is only one person who really likes me. It's my sister because she listens to me, she does not get angry. She is just a calm little sister. Whenever I get told off she helps me. My brother tells lies even if I don't hit him but my sister is always a witness. My dad believes her because she never tells fibs but my brother tells fibs. My sister is supportive, she believes me because I'm the oldest. She doesn't respect Naman because he is the youngest and he never tells the truth, so she respects the oldest and that's me, and that's how she respects me.

Here Imran's uses the word 'respect'. Within the Asian family, the prestige of the family and respect for elders is almost unanimously regarded as being inviolable and is an important part of the cultural value system. Respect is important between children and parents as well as between brothers and sisters, even if the age gap is small. In Imran's family, his father commanded respect by virtue of his gender, age and position as head of the household. He made the family decisions, played a major part in family discipline, organized family life and was highly involved in the children's school work:

> *Interviewer*: Who do you think is the boss in your house?
> *Imran*: Oh it's my dad because he is the oldest and he bought the house. He tells us what to do most of the time. My mum never tells me what to do. My dad tells me good things to do. He bought the things like footballs, he brings books for me. I say he is the boss.

Imran regarded his father as the head of the family and the chief decision-maker which mirrors the tendency for traditional Asian families to be author-itarian and patriarchal in structure. In comparison, mothers are ascribed a subordinate and submissive position which is legitimized by the claim that it is 'part of the culture' (Drury, 1991).

Alongside respect for his father, Imran keenly felt any injustices in the way his father dealt with problems between himself and his brother or sister, especially when he was accused of lying. On the other hand, he appreciated the attention he received on his school and sporting successes, when he would be rewarded, sometimes financially but always with affection:

> *Interviewer*: What happens if you have done something good?
> *Imran*: First of all my mum gives me a kiss . . and she takes me to shops and gets me some new clothes. My dad gives me money, about twenty pounds . . . my mum, she's always proud of me, and so's my dad but whenever my sister or my friends hear they are always amazed that I have done good.

Rewards for success were not the only special times in the family which Imran particularly enjoyed. He remembered several special occasions which were celebrated by family outings when both Asian and English venues would be used. This gives some insight into the way Imran's family life incorporates dimensions of contemporary Asian, as well as British, culture:

> I remember two years ago . . there was a wedding in a restaurant. My dad took my mum to the restaurant Ubdal, you know. Have you heard of it? Yeah, and he bought her food and then he gave her some flowers and chocolates. And last year, urm, my dad, you know, I had some friends from school and they took, and I went to the Mex you know, bowling, ten pin bowling and . . . and Laser Quest, you know guns, and you play on the guns . . [we] had some burgers and chips and it was a very good day that day. A very sunny day, very happy day.

When asked to speculate about family life when he was older, Imran expressed a wish to look after his parents once they get old. Emphasis on internal family support structures is a customary feature of traditional Asian culture and Imran was keen to follow this custom. In doing so, he saw an opportunity to show his respect, love and duty to this parents:

> *Interviewer*: When you grow up, describe what you want your family to be like?
> *Imran*: When I grow up I want to have two girls and one boy. I'd like to have a wealthy house. I'd like mum and dad to be happy because I buy them a new house, you know, to live in, because they would like be about sixty or seventy when I grow up. I like them to be happy when I grow up and I want them to be there so that they can have a new house and new car and everything new, whatever they want, I buy. That's it.

Imran's family life was one of perceived wealth and privilege. Despite having relatively little time with either parent on a day-to-day basis, he did not express any upset about this and reiterated his pride in his father's occupational status and hard work. His parents certainly helped him to feel valued within the family and he seemed to enjoy his family life very much. During the interview Imran gave little indication of being integrated within the local English culture, rather he upheld Asian family values and associated mainly with the local Asian community. The question of whether maintenance of the Asian culture could be a reaction to the experience of racism was not mentioned by Imran, but it is very important to remind the reader not to unduly elevate 'the role of Asian "culture" at the expense of an analysis which addresses racism' (Priestley, 1995, p. 161). Imran did not report any family conflicts based on clashes between Asian and English culture, but his account indicates a strong feeling among his family that preservation of specific cultural identity is extremely important to them.

Meena

Meena was a 15-year-old girl at the time of the interview. She had two sisters, one older, Shilpa aged 16, and one younger, Shamina aged 11. Her parents were of Indian origin, but they lived in Kenya before migrating to England. Meena's family live in a semi-detached house, one part of which is a newsagency owned and run by her parents. The house was built near a village on a busy main road. Meena and her sisters went to school by public transport, since the school was a few miles away from her home. Her grandparents lived nearby, but she could only see them during weddings and religious ceremonies due to the commitments of school work and helping in the newsagent.

Meena presented herself as a lively teenager with interests in clothes, music and outings with friends. However, she expressed far greater difficulty reconciling two systems of values and expectations than Imran. Meena had absorbed the religious and cultural values of her family, but she felt frustrated in her attempts to develop her own personal identity in ways which incorporated her experience of British cultural norms and expectations. Despite these misgivings, Meena perceives her family to be a close unit in which she felt secure, loved and cared for:

> *Interviewer*: . . . Tell me all the words that come into your head, when you think of the word 'family'.
> *Meena*: Close, loving, supportive, listening.
> *Interviewer*: Tell me all the words that come into your head when you think of the word 'home'.
> *Meena*: Safe place where you know you can come back to.
> *Interviewer*: . . . What it is like to live in a family?
> *Meena*: It's nice to have people always around you. To know people care, people want you around, lots of love and bonding. They are there when we need each other.

There are certain things about her parents' attitude of which Meena disapproved, but at the same time she was able to consider things from their point of view. She recognized the role and significance of culture as a determinant of restrictions imposed upon her by her parents. However, Meena believed that her parents are sometimes unable to understand her needs and aspirations because they do not appreciate ways in which her experience of cultural values differs from their own:

> *Interviewer*: What you don't like about your family?
> *Meena*: My parents not trusting us. Not listening to how we feel like as teenagers. It is due to our culture. They were brought up in India, and I've been brought up in England, and influenced by English people and their backgrounds and lifestyle. My parents try to understand, but I don't think they understand as well as I'd like them to . .
> *Interviewer*: Can you not explain to them?
> *Meena*: I tried and explained once, but they still keep on coming back to culture, how we should be, especially girls. How boys are different from girls. What is not allowed. If they got out more and saw what it was like, they might understand a bit better. I can't blame them for not wanting to be like that. But I wish they would understand.

When questioned about her best friend's family, Meena expressed the view that her best friend's family is completely different. She felt her best friend's parents were more understanding and supportive than her own parents who, she again stressed, found it difficult to accept her. As she explained:

> Both our families have different backgrounds. My best friend is English. My parents' and her parents' occupations are different. I think my friend's family is a bit more supportive, but they do have similar sort of standards. Her parents listen and talk to each other freely about any subject. They are a lot more outgoing. I suppose they have better understanding between them than us. Her parents try to come down to the children's level and understand.

Meena worked with her mother doing various things in the house and shop but she had little chance to go out with her mother because the home and family business had to take priority. Thus, the time mother and daughter actually spent together was monopolized by domestic duties and shop work unless family celebrations were underway:

> *Interviewer*: What kind of things do you usually do together with your mother?
> *Meena*: My mum, well we don't get to go out, but we do work together in the shop, cook, watch TV, clean, basic things in the house together a lot. We go to weddings together and special occasions like that.

Similarly, Meena's time with her father was spent mostly in the shop or accompanying him to buy stock:

> *Interviewer*: What kind of things do you usually do together with your father?
> *Meena*: The most is going to work, like Cash and Carry or working in the shop with him, sometimes we go to town together.

In contrast to these rather limited interactions with her parents, Meena did many things together with her older sister. She enjoyed her sister's company and felt able to communicate openly with her. The relationship she had with her sister came across as very supportive and understanding:

> I like having my sister, we get to talk about each other and our problems. We do everything together, go out, housework, working in shop, going to town, party, bowling, cinema.

Meena was less complimentary about her younger sister who she described as domineering to everyone else in the house:

> *Interviewer*: Who do you think is the boss in your house?
> *Meena*: My little sister.
> *Interviewer*. Why do you think?
> *Meena*: She shouts at everyone when she gets the chance, tells them

what to do, what not to do. She smacks and she picks at them. She
tries to be on top of everyone else. She doesn't like to be small.
Interviewer: What about daddy and mummy?
Meena: Well no, not really. My dad sort of plays along with her.

Even though the youngest girl in the family was reported to get away without reprimand for being bossy in the house, Meena said the older girls had
to follow the rules in the family. Discipline in the family was described as
extremely strict, especially for the older girls. In many Asian families, the
restriction imposed on girls becomes stricter as they reach maturity. Rana
(1995), for example, has shown how Asian fathers in Britain often apply traditional disciplines to their daughters. Daughters are positioned as symbol-
izing the honour and prestige ('izzat') of the family and Asian fathers are
traditionally anxious to avoid any risk of jeopardizing their marriage prospects
(Rana, 1995). In Meena's situation, when she had done something deemed
unacceptable within her family, she was directed towards her religious beliefs
and her parents required her to seek forgiveness from God:

> *Interviewer*: What happens if you do something wrong and you get
> found out?
> *Meena*: The last time was to do with school when I came home, my
> mum had a go at me, shouting, then she calmed down. I explained
> to her what happened. She talked to me, she told me why, what was
> wrong and why I shouldn't have done it. She told me to pray every
> morning for a week or so, if I am ever in trouble to remember God
> and to pray to him. I was banned from TV and going out for a bit.

Although Meena acknowledged her parents' support, she was not comfortable
in asking for it. She had a well-developed support network around her, older
sister, friends and relations. This again reflects an emphasis on the wider family network, and the importance of close-knit relationships characterized by
obedience to family norms and respect for elders which is highly valued within
Meena's own family:

> *Interviewer*: If you got upset about something, who would you talk to?
> *Meena*: I talk to my older sister about things, but not my parents that
> much. I hear about my friends, they talk to their mums more easily
> than I could talk to my mum. Probably because we never spent that
> much time when we were younger. I try to talk to her but I can't go
> into deep things about how I feel. She does care for me. She helps
> when I've got a problem, she is very helping and supportive that way.
> But I think my sister is better than my mum. She is very supportive.
> I have an uncle I can talk to him. He is in his twenties. So he is quite
> our age like. I get on well with him. If I have a problem I can talk to
> him. Otherwise I talk to my auntie . . my mum's sister. Also, I like all

my friends and get on with most of them. My best friend understands me pretty well and I can talk to her, but my mum doesn't like her.

Of course, we do need to be careful here not to recycle stereotypical images of strong support invariably being available within all Asian families. Begum (1992a, 1992b) and Shah (1992) challenge such an assumption. It is important to recognize that Meena herself is pointing out that complete support is not available within her family.

Meena's parents appreciate her educational success, but she felt that she was never given any special reward for it. There is clearly a difference in family response to educational achievement with respect to the experiences of Meena and Imran which may indicate particular gender-related expectations within their respective families:

Interviewer: What happens if you have done something good?
Meena: They are pleased, they are happy. They don't do anything special for me. They just say, 'Well done' and 'Keep it up'. Then they just carry on with what they're doing, but I would like them to notice that I have tried and I've done well. Probably celebrating some way would be nice.

Celebrations revolved around special family occasions which were enjoyed at home, and incorporated aspects of both British and Asian culture. Special occasions usually involved Asian food as Meena's father preferred home cooking. Here we again see that meals provide scope for cultural maintenance within the family, when parties otherwise take on a more universal cultural flavour:

Interviewer: What kind of special occasions have happened in your family that you can remember?
Meena: We had a 21st birthday party for my uncle, which I remember. There have been lots of weddings, my little cousin's birthdays, niece and nephew's birthdays. I enjoyed my dad's 40th birthday party.
Interviewer: What did you do?
Meena: We had a surprise party.
Interviewer: Really?
Meena: The shop and house was separate at that time. So we all managed to sneak all our family and friends into the house, and kept dad in the shop all day. When he came in we surprised him, everyone said greetings. It was fun that day. We played music, played some games. My dad talked to his friends, a bit to drink, we ate. Everything was cooked at home, dad doesn't like having outside foods.

Many of the comments Meena made suggested she was struggling to attain personal autonomy and her own identity as a young adult of Asian origins living in Britain. As other young Asian women have spelt out (Rana, 1995), Meena was keen to bring contrasting values of which she had experience closer together, rather than to see Asian versus British ways of life as incompatible. Some of her aspirations militate against the beliefs and demands of her family, for example, her wish for independence and a sense of control over her own adult destiny. She also expressed her concern about the likelihood of her having an arranged marriage and that she would want to be involved in both the choice and decision with regards to her partner. She suspected that any control she might have over her marriage plans would involve reaching a compromise with her parents:

> *Interviewer*: When you grow up, describe what you want your family to be like.
> *Meena*: To let me do what I want, and to make my own mistakes, let me lead my own life how I wish, not to interfere, but understand what I am doing . . . as long as I have a say in who I marry. I wouldn't like to just marry who they think is right.

Her reservations about marriage echo her concerns about the general restrictions her parents imposed on her with regards to mixing with the opposite sex and socializing. Again, she felt constrained by the convention within her family which were highly protective towards their daughters and allow them little freedom. Her parents exerted their control by asking a lot of questions in order to monitor her activities and relationships beyond the family. They also insisted that her sister went with her wherever she went, and the curtailing of Meena's freedom caused some resentment:

> I don't like how my parents don't wish to let me or my sisters have boyfriends or go out to late night parties. They don't trust us enough. We know why we mix and what to do and what not do, but if they could just let us go out and show them that we can do it on our own, and not go behind their backs or anything . . I'd like to come home and say, 'Seen this guy and might be going out' whatever, but I don't think that would ever happen . . . If I go out it's with my sister, but my parents always know where I am, who's there, what they're like. [Say] my friends invite me to their sleep-over, [my parents] are always wanting to know what the girls are like or whose going to be there, if there's boys and stuff like that. In our culture you have to be pure and you shouldn't have anything to do with boys until you get married. They don't like me mixing with boys. I go to girls' school so I don't get to mix with boys that much anyway.

At this point, the interviewer interjected with a comment that attempted to provide some justification for Meena's parents' beliefs, but Meena was not dissuaded from making it very clear that she felt the attitudes of her parents were unjustly burdensome:

Interviewer: I understand your point, but the thing is, mixing and sleeping are two different things . . . so being friendly doesn't . .
Meena: They don't mind me talking to boys but if [father] thinks that we are going out together or something, then he bans it . . bans us straight away he says, 'You are not to go out and see these people.' Or, if they know one of my friends are going out with boys and they have been out or they're doing things which they don't approve of, then they don't like me mixing with them.

The constraints of the culture and the limits of the extent to which girls in Asian families in Britain can behave in an autonomous manner can obviously be experienced as oppressive and have disabling effects on the development of personal identity. Threats to identity are experienced when a teenager like Meena is obliged to reconcile conflicting inducements from family and home, wider social influences such as school and peer groups, and individual needs for personal well-being (Breakwell, 1986, 1992). Clearly there is a need for support from both within and beyond the family.

Asian Family Life: Children's Perspectives

Imran and Meena both belong to Asian families living in Britain but their experiences are quite different in respect of many variables, including religion (Muslim versus Hindu), social status (professional versus working class), age (pre-teenage versus teenage) and sex (male child versus female child). This reaffirms the importance of resisting racial stereotypes when addressing children's home and family life.

Meena appears to feel 'suspended' between two worlds (Modgil, 1986) and knows aspects of her personal identity are threatened by her exposure to contrasting cultures. Imran emphasizes affinity with his own cultural group and does not dwell on his wider experiences of inclusion (or exclusion) beyond the family. Gender and age are likely to be critical variables in respect of these differences. As a boy, Imran is offered far more freedom than Meena; whereas he spends much time alone or with friends and can literally go 'to the forest and play', Meena explains that because she is a girl she is constantly in the company of her parents or sister and, if not, faces a barrage of questions about exactly what she is doing, with whom, where and so on. That Meena is more troubled by the control her family exert over her than Imran is, can come as no surprise, since she is stifled and restrained in ways with which he has never had to contend. Also, as the oldest of the two children interviewed, Meena is better equipped than Imran to reflect critically on her position. It should be noted, too, that during teenage years, conformity to parental norms is often disputed, as we see in various chapters in this book.

It is difficult to steer clear of stereotyped assumptions about the children's reflections presented in this chapter, partly because much of what they say reproduces stereotypical images. It is important, however, to consider the implications of some of the impressions the children have given. Imran, for example, is untroubled about his mother's prolonged absence when she is looking after Zarina, but the reader may like to consider whether service providers have employed racist stereotypes to explain away a lack of professional support for the family in respect of this. Similarly, Meena identifies a range of family life issues which she finds difficult to handle, but myths about the strength of 'the Asian family system' create barriers which may make it difficult for her to seek out help outside of the family.

Reviewing the experiences of Imran and Meena required all of us as writers to re-examine our own assumptions about children in Asian families living in Britain, regardless of whether or not we have personal links with minority cultural and linguistic groups. If children in Asian families living in Britain are to be comfortable about themselves in respect of their diverse experiences of culture, then it would seem important that they are encouraged to develop their own identities without pressure. Parents, and those who support families facing such issues, need to recognize that children's experience of Asian and British culture will offer a range of new possibilities and opportunities for cultural maintenance and identity, hitherto untried. Baker (1995) suggests to parents of bicultural children that all they can do is 'provide the conditions in which an individual makes up their own mind about [their] future', and likens the role of supportive adults to that of a gardener hoping to provide an optimal environment for nurture and growth. Given that the United Nations' Convention gives all children the right to personal integrity and freedom, we would like to conclude by endorsing the model of parental support which Baker (1995) proposes.

Acknowledgments

Thanks to Baljit Rana and Jaya Rout for their useful comments and suggestions on the original version of this chapter.

Thinking Points

- Visit a school and either through talking to children or observation, consider the pressures children are facing to develop a particular kind of cultural identity. What cultural images are presented within the school though displays, children's work, notices and so on? How is cultural diversity supported within the school? What cultural biases and expectations do you note? What practical measures can the school take to celebrate cultural diversity and why is this important?

- Talk to a teenager you know, or a small group of teenagers, about their views of cultural diversity in their local community. Discuss different personal experiences of being in a minority group as well as the reflections given by the children in this chapter. What advice would they give to Meena about some of the dilemmas she is facing? What would they say to Imran to prepare him for increased consciousness of cultural diversity that he may face as he goes through adolescence? Why is it that Meena's and Imran's peers are more likely to provide meaningful insights into these questions than adults?

• Taking the role of a parent of a child living in a minority cultural group in Britain, imagine that you were required to help raise awareness of the support that children in this situation might need. Draw up a plan of points which you would wish teachers to think about. How would the points you wanted to get across differ if you were talking to children from the majority cultural group? What points would you want to make to other parents who may not previously have reflected on such issues?

• How can you find out more about the experiences of children living in minority groups in Britain?

Chapter 8

Children's Experiences in Transnational Families

Kathleen Knowles and Judith Sixsmith

Introduction

In society today, more and more families are on the move. The free movement of workers between member states of the European Community is encouraging families to move to where better work opportunities exist. Firms extend their business activities into other countries and employees relocate into these new branches. The effect of such moves on the families involved has not been examined closely. In particular, although exposure to unfamiliar cultural influences is widely acknowledged to be stressful (Furnham and Bochner, 1986), little is known about the consequences for children who move with their families from one country to another.

The experiences of children who move with their families from the country of their birth to live in another country can be both enriching and disadvantageous at the same time. Moreover, the impact of the move can vary greatly from child to child. For some children, the transition from one culture to another is better than for other children. The circumstances that produce the move in the first place, conditions in the new living environment and the child's personality itself are all likely to affect the child's experience for better or for worse. So much is obvious. What we don't know is what it is like from the children's point of view, and we feel that we should know.

We believe it is our responsibility to be aware of the effects of political and economic changes on the children in our society. Because children do not experience these uprootings in the same way as adults, we need to know what children themselves say about adapting to life with their families in their new countries. Children's development can be crucially affected by early experiences, so there are sound professional and political reasons for exploring children's perspectives on transnational families.

Kathleen Knowles had some experience of a similar move back to the UK, when her youngest child was seven, after more than twenty years in Spain with her own family. She remembered some of the problems well, just as some of the advantages of the move are very clear. So far as this book was concerned, this was something of a double-edged sword: at least we knew that we were not starting the research for this chapter from a completely naive position, but the possibility that a personal bias might creep into the writing would have to be guarded against. What completely convinced us of the need to collect children's accounts of their experiences was that, over the years since Kathleen moved to the UK, she has often been surprised, sometimes shocked and upset, and at other times gratified, to learn from her own children what it was like for them. They are a close family. They communicate. She thought she knew.

We started the research for this chapter by contacting four families that we knew who fitted the 'transnational' criteria, i.e., with children that had been born and brought up for part of their childhood in one country, then had moved with their families to live in another country. Kathleen arranged pilot interviews with children in two of the families. At this point we had a rough interview schedule loosely structured around issues that we anticipated might be important, based on Kathleen's own experience, literature and conversations over the years with others who had had similar experiences. The pilot interviews would show how far the original schedule might have to be revised before embarking on the two main interviews. Kathleen conducted the interviews for this chapter as she is bilingual English/Spanish, has a working knowledge of French and Italian, and has experience of working with children in a bilingual context where English was the second language. So, to a certain extent, she felt prepared for interviewing children whose spoken English was not perfect. However, we were concerned about touching on areas that were potentially upsetting for the children. We hoped to get detailed accounts of their experiences, but were conscious of the need to listen carefully to the children's reactions during the interview to determine whether to follow a point or drop it. Sensitivity and good judgment were required both in the interviews and in the writing of this chapter.

Pilot interviews, with Pierre, a French boy aged 10 and Victoria, a Spanish girl aged 15, proved invaluable in setting the agenda for the research. After judicious efforts to create a relaxed atmosphere, and to provide explanations about the project, the children became interested in their contribution and talkative, especially once they became aware of the informal nature of the session and their freedom to talk openly about themselves and their family. Kathleen became more confident of her ability to manage communication effectively when the preferred language was not necessarily the same for interviewer and interviewee. Both Pierre and Victoria provided insightful and instructive reflections on transnational families. As a result, the pilot interviews proved enriching in terms of both knowledge and experience and enabled us to progress to the main study with increased focus.

The children whose accounts are central to this chapter were not known to us prior to the interviews, nor were their families. They had been contacted via links with friends and acquaintances. Both cases were similar in that both children had moved to England with their families and had never visited England before the move. However, in other respects the cases differed. The reasons for each move were different, the living conditions here in England were different, the families were different — in short, the move did not represent the same experience for the two children. Even so, their accounts do bear certain similarities, as will be seen.

We must remind readers at this juncture that the interviews give only a snapshot of a much larger complex picture. And although we have tried to stay out of camera-shot — describing the children's experiences by presenting what they themselves say about them — our shadows are there in that we have selected what has been included or left out, and how we have interpreted what the children said. Nonetheless, we feel hopeful that the stories emerge reasonably intact. On with the children's accounts, then.

Children's Reflections

Angel

The main language for the interview with Angel was English, with fairly frequent recourse to Spanish, both by Angel when his English vocabulary failed him, or by Kathleen when she wanted to ensure that both had understood each other.

Angel was 13 years old and had lived in Spain until he was 11. He had come to England two-and-a-half years ago with his father, mother, a brother aged 9 and a sister aged 7 at the time of the move. Before the move, his father owned and ran a small restaurant on the east coast of Spain, catering mostly for tourists. The business was seasonal, providing no income in the winter and this was one of the main reasons for moving to England; to set up a similar small business with a steady all-year income. In Spain, the family had lived in a fair-sized, three-bedroomed apartment 'over the shop' and the mother had helped run the restaurant, dealing with customers. She spoke good, fluent English. Angel's father was a chef and did the cooking in the restaurant, dealing less with the customers. He spoke some English but this was not fluent. The children's school in Spain was nearby and they had walked there each day by themselves, returning home at midday for their lunch. They had two paternal grandparents, an aunt and uncle and three cousins who lived in the same small town as themselves.

In England, the family lived in a small, rented, two-bedroomed semi-detached house in a suburb of a cathedral city. The restaurant was near the centre of the city but not in a prime location. It was open all the year. The younger children's Roman Catholic primary school was two bus rides away from the house and their mother escorted them in the mornings to school and collected them in the afternoons. The mother's contact with the restaurant was now minimal. Angel had spent two terms at the same primary school as his brother and sister before starting secondary education at a local state comprehensive school. He travelled there and back on a school bus. The family had no relations living in England.

Angel was pleasant, but restrained at first. However, he soon became relaxed and opened up, displaying a lively curiosity about the reasons for the research and chatting easily about himself, his family, and life in England.

One of the questions Angel was asked was what the word 'family' meant to him. His description gives a picture of a group of people feeling secure in the close links that joined them, sharing and caring for each other:

> *Interviewer*: What words come into your head when you think of the word 'family'?
> *Angel*: People you are used to being with, people who love you, er, comfortable, food, company.
>
> *Interviewer*: And 'home', what does that mean to you?
> *Angel*: A place where you feel safe, where you can relax, where all your things are.

He explained what it was like when he first came to England. Some signs of culture shock are clear:

> *Angel*: I hated it. I really did. It was awful. I didn't like it one bit.
> *Interviewer*: Uh huh. Right. Why was that?
> *Angel*: Er well oh it was just everything. The weather, the English people, the food, everything really. Not understanding anything anyone was saying. Just everything. It's hard to describe. It was my first time out of Spain . . . just all like a big mystery . . . adventure.

Other members of his family had the same initial feelings of disorientation and exhilaration, followed by let-down — his brother and sister, too, had shared this experience:

> *Interviewer*: How was it an adventure?
> *Angel*: Just everything so different . . exciting. We were all excited . . at first. Then after a bit we just wanted to go back to Spain.
> *Interviewer*: You came in the winter didn't you. Hmm yeah. What was it about English people that you didn't like?
> *Angel*: They were really serious all the time . . . really quiet. Not friendly. And you couldn't tell what they were talking about. I mean I just looked at them and thought how weird they were, they just stood still talking and didn't move their arms or anything.
> *Interviewer*: Were they all unfriendly?
> *Angel*: No, no, they were nice, well they tried to be nice, I think, but . . . oh . . . it was just that you didn't know what they were saying, talking about.

And regarding the first weeks of primary school in England, Angel described the immersion experience thus:

I didn't like being in a crowd of people and not understand anything at all. So it was like being in a room where you couldn't hear because you didn't understand anything. I didn't take any notice of the people round me because it was just like, Wow! I don't understand anything. I just pretended all the time.

Angel and his siblings did not at first have any contact with English children of their own age except during school hours. This exclusion from an important arena for childhood social activities (play, conversations with friends, etc.) had an effect on Angel's emotional state that lingered for a considerable time, in that he felt isolated and unhappy:

Angel: I felt awkward.
Interviewer: Uh huh.
Angel: That's about it, I felt awkward all the time. I didn't want to er .. I couldn't like do things like .. there wasn't anything I could do at first.
Interviewer: Do?
Angel: I couldn't play out, I couldn't understand what they were saying on the telly, I couldn't go anywhere .. oh .. hm.
Interviewer: Hm. How long was it like this?
Angel: Well, erm, for quite a bit really. A few months.

This was despite overtures made by children from neighbouring houses in the street where he lived, who knocked on the door to invite him and his siblings out to play. He said that although they wanted to join in the neighbourhood children's activities, which they watched through the window from inside the house, they feared that their inability to communicate would thwart any attempts to integrate themselves into the neighbourhood peer group:

Angel: We could hear them playing outside and we used to go up-stairs and watch them from the window in mum's bedroom. Some-times you could tell what they were playing like hide-and-seek because we have that in Spain, it's just the same in England .. well .. just different words .. like it's 'escondite' in Spain but you play it the same.
Interviewer: Uh huh. Right. So did you join in then?
Angel: Not right away, not at first. We used to dare each other to go down and join in .. but we didn't like to because .. I wanted to sometimes but then [my brother] used to say 'and if they start to play something else, then what?'
Interviewer: So is that why you didn't join in, in case the game changed?
Angel: Well then you would be out there and you wouldn't under-stand what was going on. And how could they tell you how to play it? You would just spoil it if you don't know the rules.

At this time, family provided emotional support and company for Angel. The three children provided each other with mutual support, playing together inside the house for most of the time when they were at home. Their mother played a supportive role too by suggesting activities when they ran out of ideas, such as writing letters to their relations in Spain, or drawing pictures, which was an activity that all three children enjoyed. The pictures were then saved to show to their father later. In this way, the father too, often now absent from home for business reasons, was integrated into family activities:

> *Interviewer*: So .. at this time, you know when you didn't like to go out to play, was there anything you did like to do?
> *Angel*: Umm .. we used to spend loads of time drawing when we didn't go out a lot. We're all quite good at drawing in my family. I'm best but I'm the oldest [*laughs*]. My mum used to say, 'Why don't you draw something, why don't you do some pictures?'
> *Interviewer*: So your mum used to suggest doing some drawing?
> *Angel*: Sometimes we just used to do it ourselves.
> *Interviewer*: Uh huh.
> *Angel*: We throw away any rubbish ones and keep the good ones to show to dad . . . He loves looking at our pictures. He says, 'Oh, that's *good*, that's excellent. Keep it up.' He takes some of them to work and shows them to people.
> *Interviewer*: Oh, that's nice. They must be good.
> *Angel*: Mine are usually. My sister she does a lot of rubbing out but he still takes them, sometimes, and [my brother's].

Angel's parents helped him and his brother and sister to find the courage to go out and make friends with the neighbours' children. They attempted to diminish the threat of the first encounters in various ways. They commented on how nice and friendly the children seemed in making the first moves towards establishing a friendship. They also pointed out that Angel and his brother and sister could always come back into the house if they found they did not like to be out in the street playing with the other children. The mother, in particular, went further. Angel told me how, at Angel's request, she agreed that, the first time that the children did go out to play with their neighbours, if things were not going well, she would pretend that she wanted them to come back into the house. So, with the safe refuge of their home and family close by, Angel and his siblings felt confident enough to venture forth and forge the first links of friendships:

> *Interviewer*: So when did you .. how did you eventually start playing out?. Can you tell me about that?
> *Angel*: Well .. my sister she really wanted to go out and play with the others .. she used shout 'Hello' out of the front door and then run back in. And I wanted to go out because I was really bored . . . But

. . oh . . we still thought that . . oooh . . [*wriggles and screws up face*] we just didn't have enough . . [courage]. So [my brother] said he would go out with us if we would come back in again straight away if we got in a mess. So we said to mum we were going to knock on the front door and pretend to ask her something if we wanted to come back in and she had to tell us to come in and tell them we had to stay in.

Interviewer: Uh huh. And what did your mum say to that?

Angel: At first she said we were just being silly, she said, 'Just go out and make friends with them,' but we all said, 'Please, please, please,' and she said 'OK'.

Interviewer: And is that what happened, did it work?

Angel: Umm . . actually, I think we just used to knock and ask her what they were saying . . . it was OK really.

Although it took quite some time for Angel and his siblings to voluntarily approach neighbours' children at home, later in the interview Angel recounts how at school he started joining in the playtime games only a couple of weeks after starting primary school:

At first we [he and his siblings] just stood there and talked to each other and watched the others playing. But then after a couple of weeks you sort of see what they're playing and you start running around with them. And if it's football that's easy. I was always goalie because I could really dive for the ball.

Nonetheless, the feeling 'awkward' state endured until 'just being able to speak the language' changed things for him.

Meanwhile, although his family was a source of emotional support, the company of others striving to learn English (his siblings) and a mother who could speak good English apparently did little to speed Angel's acquisition of English:

Interviewer: Did the rest of the family make it any better for you?

Angel: Well er I suppose maybe. We talked about it and told each other new words. And if I wanted to know how to say something or how to pronounce something I wasn't sure of I asked my mother. But we spoke Spanish at home so it was OK there. My dad wanted my mum to teach us English at nights but we didn't like it and she didn't either, so we didn't. We just relaxed when we were at home.

Going to school had helped Angel to learn English, not because there had been strenuous efforts on the part of the school to help Angel, but mainly in his interactions with the other pupils who would go at a pace that he could keep up with:

Angel: The other kids. Yeah, they, er, well what happened was they'd talk slowly to me and if I said something wrong they'd kind of say 'No that's not how you say it' and they'd tell me how to say it. It was a laugh sometimes. Hey yeah, like when I couldn't say 'chips' and I used to practise in the dinner queue.
Interviewer: Did you have any special English lessons at school?
Angel: No.
Interviewer: Would things have been better if you had?
Angel: No it would have made me feel different to the other kids.
Interviewer: So was there any help from the school or the teacher or did you just have to pick it up on your own?
Angel: Well the first teacher I had he gave me some questionnaires to write out and I had to keep writing out the words I didn't know and that made me remember them. That was OK but mostly it was just picking it up.

Angel gives us an insight into how his desire to be no different from his classmates and the advantage to be gained from additional English lessons might have been reconciled. It was clear that Angel did not want to be taken out of his peer group for separate English classes:

If they'd have given us special lessons after school that would have been better. I think that I wouldn't still be behind like I am if they'd done that. . . . I am behind in English literature and English language but that's only normal. It's not that, it's other subjects where you just don't understand what they want you to do.

Only when Angel had sufficient grasp of English to find reading or watching television enjoyable did these media play any part in increasing Angel's command of English. His account gives us a vivid illustration of how the family together coped with watching television in English:

Interviewer: And what about after school, did you watch television?
Angel: Yeah sometimes, specially if it was bad the weather and we couldn't play out.
Interviewer: Did watching television help you to learn English?
Angel: Not at first because we couldn't understand anything that was going on. We used to watch the cartoons they were OK and my little sister used to laugh really loud and she didn't understand anything and she couldn't tell what was a commercial. She just watched the pictures and she didn't understand any of it at first. Sometimes mum would translate for us if she wasn't busy. But that doesn't really work because you can't hear what they're saying next. We didn't really enjoy it at first for ages. Yeah, now it's good. You learn a lot of English from the telly.

Interviewer: And reading?
Angel: Now I do, I read a lot. But not at first, no way.

Angel returned to the experience of changing to a school in a new country. It was clear that this had opened up possibilities for him, for example, in forming friendships with English children of his own age and in learning English. But even after the first few difficult months, when the lack of English had been the major problem, he still found differences in teaching style, school regime and interpersonal relations between teachers and pupils difficult to accommodate. He began to refer to the concept of 'respect' in these contexts.

Angel saw the high degree of respect displayed by pupils to teachers in Spain as part of the respect towards adults in general across the wider Spanish society, and especially towards all adults within the family:

Interviewer: What about school? What do you think of school?
Angel: Well I didn't like it at first and I still don't like it as much as I did in Spain. [*Here Angel is referring to both his primary school and secondary school in England*]
Interviewer: Why is that?
Angel: Oh erm, it's not the same. They're er not friendly the . . teachers and . . the classes the kids don't take part as much, they're not as lively . . they don't all join in and they don't get you up to the blackboard to do say fractions or decimals if you got the right answer.

Angel perceived the regime at his secondary school as more hierarchical and punitive than in Spain:

Interviewer: Is it different in Spain?
Angel: Oh yes . . here . . . erm, well it's just different. They're up there and you are here and they don't treat you the same. They're very strict and er like regimental. You get punished too much for things that don't matter, that are nothing really.

Angel showed strong preference for the approach that he was accustomed to in Spain, based on dialogue between teacher and pupil, and appeals by the teacher to the pupil's sense of right and wrong, cross-referenced to notions of family:

Interviewer: What do you think should have happened?
Angel: A telling off, er get sent out, stand outside in the corridor. Or have to stand up near a teacher. You would have to say you're sorry and ask to be forgive . . . In Spain they sort it out more . . . they talk to you more about it and they make you feel sorry, you know . . . When you're talking in class, they tell you off, they say you should be grateful because your parents had to pay for all their education . . .

they tell you that when you are grown up you won't have a job and your family will go hungry . . . My Dad says it too. He says that we'll only have raw onion to eat if we don't work [at school].

Angel's explanations indicated a belief that this approach to discipline could not easily be implemented in his English school, because it was underpinned by feelings of 'respect' towards teachers. Here, he is recognizing that the cultural background to interpersonal relations plays a major part in what is, and what is not, possible in such communications.

Interviewer: Is this how you would like things to be done?
Angel: Yes but it wouldn't work here . . . There's no respect for the teachers and the kids wouldn't take any notice of a telling off. They'd think, 'Brilliant, I got away with it.'

The family is where children learn the first ideas of respect for older people (i.e., anyone older than oneself) which seems to be part of the fabric of Spanish society. They learn this vicariously by observing the behaviour of their parents towards older people, and by instruction from their parents and other caregivers when they are small children. This learning is reinforced by attitudes in society as the children begin to move in wider circles outside of the family. Regarding why one should have respect for one's parents, Angel responded simply 'Just because they are your parents.' He felt that anyone who behaves with a lack of respect towards an older person is likely to be censured by the rest of society.

Despite those aspects of English society and the educational system that Angel was uncomfortable with, and the belief that the change to another language still held him back in certain subjects, Angel and his family had reasons to be glad, overall, about the move to an English school. The prospect of becoming fluent in two languages was one reason, the educational facilities at the secondary school another. For example, the family discussed and rejoiced in the wide availability of skills training in English schools. These discussions had obviously led Angel to value the educational opportunities at his school. Listing the subjects that he currently studied, Angel talked about certain subjects that might not have been readily available to him if he had stayed in Spain, and which he obviously enjoyed very much:

We do computer studies and I can type quite fast now. I can easily beat some of my friends except Jason because he has got a computer at home. Mr Brown [the teacher] said I am doing very well. It's dead easy for me. It's one of my favourite subjects. And woodwork and metalwork. I'm good at them too. You don't do them in Spain like you do here. You would have to pay to learn computers in Spain.

His parents were also keen for Angel to do well academically, with a view to an English university education, which they had told him was a passport to a secure, prosperous future. There had been tensions in the family regarding academic progress, especially related to the acquisition and practice of the English language. Angel's mother did not wish English to usurp Spanish as the main family language, whereas his father saw English as a prerequisite for progress and so made what Angel saw as bothersome demands of his family:

> *Interviewer*: Your mum speaks good English doesn't she? Was that a help when you first arrived?
> *Angel*: Yeah not really erm sometimes. Well when we were at home she would tell us things but we we doesn't talk to us in English. Except when one of our friends comes. She said we'll forget how to speak Spanish.
> *Interviewer*: What about your dad? Did he help you to learn English?
> *Angel*: He says English is very important for school. He always wants us to speak English to him. Like at breakfast he's always testing us. I can't say things properly when he's making us do it. He thinks we can't speak English very well and loads of times when I'm talking to my friends I don't even have to think of the words . . . but he's never around when our friends are here. He didn't go to university and he says that we are going to. He wanted mum to teach us English at home but we didn't.

Angel's mother acted as mediator between the children and the father in this situation, in turn supporting and explaining the views of each side:

> Mum tells him that we can speak it really well . . . She says he just wants us to get on and do well.

The move to England had resulted in changes in living conditions that the whole family had difficulty in getting used to, including Angel's parents. The house they were renting here in England was much smaller, with only two bedrooms, than the apartment that was their home in Spain. The living room now doubled as a bedroom for Angel's parents. Both parents were having to come to terms with a sharp separation of roles and activities that once had been shared. Because their present house was at some distance from their restaurant, and because Angel's mother accompanied the younger children to and from primary school each day, she could no longer help with the business as she had been able to do in Spain, living as they did then 'over the shop'. One way that these changes affected the family was by upsetting the mother, whose patience with the children became shorter. Angel felt that his mother snapped at them more than when they lived in Spain. Another effect of these changes was that Angel's father worked long hours away from home and now had little time to spend with his family, apart from breakfast times:

> Well we erm dad's at work most of the time. It's mum mostly because he has to be there. He's a chef you know. He's gone to work when

we get back home and he works weekends as well. It was nicer in Spain. Dad used to play with us and we used to go out all over the place.

The children gave emotional support to the parents during this difficult period of adjustment. Angel said that he and his brother and sister worried that their mother was unhappy about living in England. On occasions she had openly expressed her regret at having moved to England, although on the other hand she agreed with her husband that the move would benefit the children. Angel explained that when she appeared to be sad or unhappy, the children would try cheer her up. This might involve, for example, asking her what was the matter, hugging her, sometimes doing small chores unasked, or 'not bothering her', i.e., not going to her with their troubles when she appeared to feel low:

> *Angel*: We used to think that she was sad, sometimes, like if she was quiet. She still is sometimes.
> *Interviewer*: And how do you feel when you see you mum is quiet? What do you do?
> *Angel*: I say, 'What's the matter . . are you feeling sad . . don't you feel well?' I tell the others to be quiet . . . we do surprises for her . . make her a coffee . . be really quiet and do our bedrooms or something. My sister sits on her knee and hugs her round her neck.
> *Interviewer*: Uh huh.
> *Angel*: And we try to be really good and not bother her . . . like not tell her about things that might worry her.
> *Interviewer*: Like what sort of things?
> *Angel*: Umm, being in trouble at school, not being friends with some-one any more.

They are also aware of the father's increased work burden and show forbearance by not making demands on him for time and attention:

> When he has time off now he's tired and anyway it's too dark or it's too cold or something . . . He would like to but he is very busy.

Another part of their past life in Spain that Angel missed was the company of his relations who lived in the same town. He said that he and his brother and sister used to go and stay with his relations when his parents were busy with the restaurant in the height of the summer tourist season. Their grandparents, aunt, uncle, and cousins would all decamp for a month to a small village about seventy miles (100 kilometres) inland, from where the grandparents originated and where they still had a house. Various more distant relations lived in the village. This summer exodus was one of the high spots of the children's life, with older and younger generations enjoying a simple but very relaxed lifestyle:

All the [four] boys we all sleep together in the same room. They [the adults] take one of the mattresses off the bed and put it on the floor because there's only one big bed. We have turns.

Angel said that the first summer they spent in England was a sad time because they kept thinking of their Spanish relations and the good times they had shared. They had not seen their Spanish relations since coming to England, but had not missed them too badly after the first few weeks. Angel's younger sister, then 7 years old, had been particularly upset because she was too young to understand why they could not go to the village once school summer holidays started. Angel disclosed that when his sister was told they were not going, she cried repeatedly for her grandmother and aunt. Her distress started a ball rolling and upset the rest of the family. Eventually, between parents and children, they agreed on a series of summer 'treats' (days out, trips to the swimming baths, and so on) and spirits lifted.

Angel had reached a stage where he felt reasonably good about living in England and optimistic about himself and his future. He had some regrets about leaving Spain but obviously felt safe and secure in his present life because of the stability and warmth of his family life.

Silvia

Silvia was a 12-year-old girl who had come from Italy to England with her mother, father and older brother (now aged 16) when she was nine. Her father was an engineer whose firm had promoted him to head of a department in its north west office. Her mother had not worked outside the home since Silvia's brother had been born, but had a wide circle of friends and relations and enjoyed a busy social life. In Italy, the family had lived in a flat in a large block of apartments in the centre of Padua. Their mother had driven them to private school each day and collected them each afternoon. The children had lunch at school each day. They had a large extended family in Padua whom they saw often, and in Verona, also in the north of Italy, from where their father originally came. They had a second home, a villa in the countryside beyond the city, where they often spent weekends and holidays, especially when the weather in Padua was hot.

In England, the family lived in a detached house on a modern housing estate in a suburb of a town near a large industrial city, in the catchment area of a secondary school with a very good reputation. Silvia had first gone to a local primary school for a year-and-a-half before joining her brother at secondary school. Silvia's brother had several good friends from school and from the gym where he practised martial arts. He spent a lot of time with his friends and was often out of the house. Silvia's father had a good working knowledge of English which he spoke at work to the English staff. He left the house in the morning with the children, dropping them at school on his way to work.

Silvia's mother had learnt some English when she was at school, but had never practised this thereafter. She now found the English language difficult to learn and to pronounce. She was attending weekly afternoon English classes at a local college of further education but making very gradual progress. She depended on her children and husband to translate for her when they went out. She did not feel confident enough to drive a car on the lefthand side of the road. As a housewife, she was much more isolated in England than in Italy.

Silvia was a quietly spoken girl. She was rather shy at first and mono-syllabic in her answers, but gradually relaxed and conversation became easy. Once she felt at ease, she was very articulate. Silvia was asked to describe what the word 'family' meant to her:

> Well, my parents and my brother, they are my family, and then there's my family in Italy but I don't see them a lot now. Family is all the people you're related to. All the people who are very close to you.

She described 'home' as being:

> Your house, your own place. It's where you feel relaxed and just be yourself and where nobody is ever going to not speak to you. There will always be somebody you can talk to.

Silvia talked about what it had been like when they first arrived in England. At first she said she could not remember a lot about it because it was all so confusing. She began to tell me what she could and the memories started to come back to her. Bit by bit, Kathleen pieced together the picture of a family whose move to England was perceived by them as prestigious, financially advantageous and offering improved educational/career prospects for the children:

> My father wanted to be head of department here because it's a bigger office than the one in Sweden [where he had spent some time and might have been promoted to]. It's more money here than in Padua . . . My parents said that they wish they could have gone to school in England or America because they would be able to speak English perfectly. They say that all really well educated people speak good English . . . My cousins in Italy say we're so lucky. We go back for Christmas and in the summer. And my cousins have been over here too and stayed with us. They're learning English.

Adjusting to life in England, however, had not been easy. Silvia had had to come to terms with the loss of her friends at primary school and the frequent contact with her relations in Italy:

> *Interviewer*: What did you think of it when you first came to England?
> *Silvia*: I was too little at first to realize what moving to England

meant. I can't remember feeling sad when I left because I didn't even think about not seeing everybody again. It was like being on holiday, except that you didn't go home again. But then I began to miss them. I didn't have any friends at first. My brother would play with me sometimes, but he made friends of his own. He likes playing football.

Silvia's mother had been sympathetic company at that point. She herself was finding life in England hard to bear. In turn, her daughter was a source of company for her, the family functioning as a support system for its members:

Interviewer: Did anything make it better for you?
Silvia: My mother used to hug me and cheer me up. She used to say only one month or two months or three months and we go to Padua. She used to find things for me to do when I was feeling like that. Sometimes she would make cakes and I would help. Sometimes we got the bus and went shopping then a taxi back. My mother loves shopping. I go with her because my father hates to go shopping. My father and brother they are both the same like that.
Interviewer: Does your mother look forward to her visits to Padua, or was she just cheering you up?
Silvia: She really doesn't like it here, but she says her place is by my father's side.

Primary school had been a mixed experience for Silvia. She recounted how in primary school she began to feel the impact of the loss of her old friends:

Interviewer: What was it like when you started at primary school?
Silvia: Not nice. I didn't understand and it was all too much for the first few months. In primary school I did not feel happy. I did not have a best friend, just a class full of people I didn't understand. Primary school I didn't like it. I always like to have a best friend, that's just what I am like.

Silvia remembered how staff and pupils made efforts to make her feel more at home:

Interviewer: Did anyone at the school do anything that made it better for you?
Silvia: Oh yes. Mr Jones [headmaster] used to take me to the front and put his arm round my shoulders and point at things in the room and if I said it right everyone would clap and cheer.
Interviewer: And did this make you feel better?
Silvia: Well yes because it made you come out of that little shell where you were in your own world and join in with everyone else. And sometimes girls would tell me to sit with them when we were making groups. So people did try to be friendly.

Silvia thought that her high profile as the only foreign pupil in the class might have been the attraction behind some of the friendly overtures made by some of the pupils. While these gestures of friendship didn't result in Silvia's finding a 'best friend', she said that it did make her feel better temporarily. On the other hand, being the centre of attention made some pupils less well disposed to her:

> I don't know if they wanted to be friends or I was more the centre of attention. I won a handwriting competition and they said it was just because I was Italian and the centre of attention.

Silvia did not feel comfortable during her year-and-a-half at primary school. She thought children of that age do not make friends 'just like that' where there is no shared language. There were also teachers who were impatient with her inability to understand. Remarks such as, 'Are you stupid? I've already told you what to do,' made Silvia feel 'thick' and unhappy at that time. Silvia still resented the unfairness of such remarks but no longer believed herself to be stupid. Regarding pupils who have little English, she said that teachers should be:

> . . Much, much, much more patient with them. They should spend more time with them and explain things slowly to them.

She did not bring the teachers' disparaging remarks to the notice of her parents because she thought that her father was very busy and worried about work and her mother was upset and used to cry when things went wrong. It was apparent that the children's role in the family support system extended to protecting the parents from further worry when the children perceived the parents to be under stress. This meant that sometimes the children tried to cope alone with difficult situations.

   Learning English for Silvia had been a question of gradual acquisition over time with school classes, interactions with pupils at school and a small group of playmates who lived in neighbouring houses. She had felt happiest in this last learning situation, where the learning was informal, where there was less pressure and home was on hand if Silvia wanted to withdraw:

> *Interviewer*: How did playing with the children who live near you help?
> *Silvia*: I really don't know how we understood each other. I remember that Michele used to get hold of me and show me what she meant and say it and make me say it too. But I don't know how we understood each other so much. We would play for hours and we must have just mimed to each other.

Secondary school was a turning point in Silvia's adjustment to life in England. Whereas primary school had not been a happy experience, secondary school was an enjoyable place to be. One reason was that it was an opportunity to start friendships without having to break into already formed friendship groups:

> *Interviewer:* What is it like now at school?
> *Silvia:* I like school now. I met Catherine, my best friend so I've got someone to lean on now. Instead of me being the new girl and the centre of attention, everyone was new, except the ones who'd all been to the same school before and already knew each other.

Silvia explained how she was enjoying doing new subjects and that her parents were quite happy with her reports. This was not the case with her brother who was heading towards GCSE exams. His parents were insisting that he should scale down his sporting activities and concentrate on his studies. This was a source of disharmony in the home. There were loud and frequent arguments between Silvia's parents and her brother on the subject of school work. Silvia felt torn between her brother and parents:

> It's awful when my father gets home. My mother tells him that my brother has done no homework and wants to go out. My brother says he's done all his homework quickly so that he can go out. They all end up shouting at each other. He gets sent upstairs and told to study. I feel sorry for him sometimes but he upsets mum. He says he's going to leave home.

Respect for parents was an issue that seemed to be important in Silvia's family. According to Silvia, this respect was owed to parents not simply by virtue of their position as parents and their superior age. Silvia thought that children should respect their parents because of the 'sacrifices' parents made for their children and in recognition of the bond of love between parents and children. Regarding some of her brother's friends, Silvia said:

> *Silvia:* Some hardly study at all. They take no notice of what their parents say.
> *Interviewer:* What do you think of that?
> *Silvia:* I think they should have more respect for their parents. Your parents make a lot of sacrifices for you and they love you and you should respect them.
> *Interviewer:* Do your friends respect their parents?
> *Silvia:* I think so.

Silvia was asked how she felt now about having moved to England. There was a mixture of feelings and opinions in her reply:

> Well I like school and I like where I live and I have loads of friends now. I still miss my family in Italy but not most of the time, usually

just when we talk about them. I definitely don't like the weather here in winter. I like the countryside in England but the weather spoils it. I like going back to Italy, but I am glad to get back here now. My mother isn't, she misses being in Italy. She would like to go back but I didn't think we will go back now until after my brother finishes university. My father likes working here.

Overall, the general impression was that she was in favour of the move. Silvia was well on the way to building a new life for herself in England, without relinquishing valued aspects of her past life in Italy. The security and support supplied by her family, even by her mother who had not yet accepted the changes to her own life, had been crucial in this process.

Transnational Family Life: Children's Perspectives

What first struck us about the accounts of the two children in the main study were certain similarities in their experiences. On the positive side, both children seemed to feel safe, secure and loved within their family environment. On the other hand, they both had struggled and were still struggling with issues related to the move from one country to another. In these struggles, family bonds could be a source of support or an added complication.

Both children had been supported by the family in the first difficult months when they started to be integrated into English society. The support had been a two-way system, with the children noticing, and trying to alleviate, their parents own struggles, sometimes by keeping their own problems from the parents' attention.

Integration into peer groups had not been quick or easy for either child. Prolonged peer rejection and peer isolation is associated with an increased risk for a range of later psychosocial and psychiatric problems (Rutter and Rutter, 1992). Their mothers especially had been available and understanding in the day-to-day problems of settling into school and had facilitated the establishment of cordial peer group relationships. And while the children were still hovering outside of their social groups, the family provided a safe haven where their sense of identity and security was reaffirmed.

In both families, the father was the sole breadwinner. Although the level of income they each generated was substantially different — Silvia's father a well-paid professional and Angel's father struggling to make a success of his restaurant business — each was perceived by his children to be hardworking and dedicated to the family welfare. Both mothers' main responsibility was to take care of the home and the family, but Angel's mother's fluency with English meant that she was less isolated and less dependent on her children and husband than Silvia's mother, whose English was poor. The better economic position of Silvia's family meant that although her mother felt isolated from English society, she had few money worries and derived comfort from fairly frequent contact with her extended family in Italy.

Differences in cultural values represented a problem for both children, manifest in their reflection on 'respect' and what they perceived as a lack of respect in English society. Although from different countries themselves, their two cultures were strikingly similar in this regard.

The acquisition of English language had been accomplished to a large degree by both children through immersion in daily living situations, which according to their accounts was an unpleasant and potentially traumatic process. Once again the family had represented a haven from the pressures they had felt when they were unable to communicate with English people. Angel felt that he was still at a disadvantage because of falling behind in his studies when he first arrived in England. The Children Act (1989) encharged local authorities with identifying and supporting children in need of help but little seems to have been done to support these children, apart from limited attempts by some teachers in the acquisition of very basic English. Tunstill, Aldgate, Wilson and Sutton (1996) point out that given the major inter- and intra-organizational and funding issues faced by local authorities, health authorities and trusts, it is not surprising that services are not looking to extend their roles in the provision of child-care services. So children from this type of family are not likely to be offered help, and their families are not likely to have the knowledge of policy background that might persuade them to pursue the provision of support.

Given that language is the key to integration and is crucially related to successful psychological adjustment to new environments (Corson, 1993; Baker, 1995), perhaps policy-makers and professionals should take heed of what children have to say about the help they need in this area. It has been suggested (Piper, 1994) that children can play a vital role in making decisions about some areas of their education, and these children's reflections indicate clearly that they would have appreciated extra language support, but not if that meant segregation from their peers.

The children's reflections reveal differences between their experiences. One interesting and typical difference was the ways in which Angel and Silvia had integrated into their peer groups: Angel by forming links with a group of boys, and Silvia by forming a close friendship with one girl (her 'best friend'). Silvia had regular direct contact with the members of her extended family in Italy, whereas Angel had not seen his relations in Spain since coming to England. Angel was the eldest of the three children in his family, while Silvia had an older sibling who was in the throes of adolescent independence struggles with the parents. The families had different levels of income and living standards. Silvia was pleased with her progress at school but Angel was dissatisfied with his level of attainment in some areas.

Overall, both children seemed to experience their families as a safe, loving focus for their life that survived intact despite the transnational uprooting. Their home provided a physical location and secure base for their social and emotional forays into their new environment. They had been able to continue the development of close relationships within and outside the family. Their school life was progressing reasonably satisfactorily with support from their families, although problem areas were discernible. Family life in these two transnational families was central to the happiness of these children, a safe haven in turbulent seas.

Thinking Points

- Children may sometimes keep their problems to themselves to shield parents who are under pressure from further distress. A transnational family is a potential scenario for this behaviour. What can professionals do to support children in this situation? Who else might offer children support in this situation? How can children be encouraged to seek such support?

- Adapting to a new environment is crucially related to the acquisition of the language of that environment. Professionals, policy-makers and parents need to listen to children to discover the most appropriate ways in which language acquisition might be speeded up. Can you think of examples of good practice? What needs to be done to encourage these?

- Children's educational progress is disrupted when they move from one country to another and from one language to another. What systems need to be set up to monitor their transition from one educational environment to another? How should children be supported through this transition in the school and in the home? How can we ensure that any support on offer is both adequate and appropriate?

- Integration into peer groups is vital for children's emotional, psychological and social development and this can be difficult for children who move from one country to another. What can professionals do to support such children in their difficulties? What can parents do? What can **you** do?

Chapter 9

Conclusions

*Michele Moore, Judith Sixsmith and
Kathleen Knowles*

In this concluding chapter, many of the threads that run through the chapters are pulled together to provide readers with an overview of the key issues concerning the children's experiences and the implications of these for social policy and professional practice. Firstly, some of the most important characteristics of the family and family life as revealed by the children's accounts are highlighted. Issues and concerns raised by the children themselves are reviewed. As the rich, qualitative detail of the children's words will necessarily be lost here, the reader is recommended to go back to the children's reflections to embellish this review. Secondly, proposals are made about how we might respond to and help children across the variety of family circumstances in which they find themselves. Thirdly, we discuss thorny methodological and ethical issues since these have shaped the research process and provide a framework through which the children's reflections can be evaluated. Finally, the implications of family-friendly policies for maximizing children's assorted experiences of family circumstances are considered.

Family Life: The Children's Experience

Despite the different family situations of the children involved in this book, it is notable that they recount similar experiences within their family life. They all derive support, love, bolsters to their self-esteem, a sense of security and a basis for self-development from belonging to a family. Throughout the trials and tribulations of their stories, the family emerges as a firm anchor in life for the children. Although there are also substantial differences in the children's perspectives, the accounts affirm that family life of whatever type, for much of the time, is a safe, secure and enjoyable experience. In this sense, the adult world's assumptions about the nuclear family as an 'ideal type' is strongly challenged. As a society, we need to accept the strengths and weaknesses of diverse family types. In the following analysis, similarities and differences, advantages and disadvantages of family life from the child's perspective are reviewed.

Definitions of the Family

An interesting starting point is to look at how children define the concept of a family. It was surprising just how eclectic children can be in the people they designate as part of their family. Definitions of family ranged beyond the boundaries of the household to wider kinship relationships, into friendships and even pets. All the children had their own reasons for including whom they did in their family and for their various reflections on what 'family' meant to them.

An important dimension of how the children defined their own families was the sense of uniqueness that accompanied each family. All the children felt that their own family was special — special because of the people in them, the activities they enjoyed together and the shared family events. Thus, the family was a place in which the children could develop their sense of personal and family identity.

Identity Within the Family

The issue of developing a sense of identity is perhaps most clearly addressed among the children from traditional, transnational, 'dual career', and Asian families. Gaining independence is one aspect of developing a sense of personal and family identity and these children were all in the process of working out their own level of independence. Support from within the family could create opportunities for increasing personal independence. This was evidently the case for Adam (traditional family), Silvia and Angel (transnational families). However, increasing independence could cause dismay and family conflict when the cultural values upheld by the family were at odds with those in the wider community. Meena (Asian family) reflected on her need for independence and how this clashed with her parents' desires to restrict her freedom in line with Asian family values pertaining to the protection of daughters.

The children spoke of other ways, too, in which they asserted their own sense of self within the family boundaries, for example, by challenging family practices. The Smith boy (multiple commitment family) was quite clear about how he did not want to fall in line with family practices concerning his disabled sister. Similarly, the Bell boy (multiple commitment family) asserted his own feelings surrounding Aunt Polly and was loath to support the family policy on this issue. In a dialectical relationship with their families, these children asserted their independence yet gained the support from which they were fashioning their sense of themselves as autonomous individuals.

Family Process and Structure

It is interesting to note that the processes that underlie family structure were similar across most of the different family types. We gather that, for all the children, families are all certainly about the give and take of everyday life. Each family had developed ways of dealing with conflict between family members, particularly concerning discipline and emotional upsets. Adam (traditional family), Imran (Asian family) and Jane (d/Deaf parents) gave good accounts of family squabbles and how they were dealt with by family members. Parents (particularly mums) and friends were the main sources of support for the children in times of emotional upset, with school teachers playing a minor role here too. Family rules and regulations are a well understood part of everyday life by most of the children who talked to us, even though the discipline they entail may be disliked (e.g., Thomas, dual career family). Each family had instituted rules and rituals which helped to support its feelings of togetherness and uniqueness. A clear example of this is Jonathan's (traditional family) description of his family's way of celebrating birthdays.

Friends and Family

It was clear from the children's accounts that family and friends were bound together in an integrated relationship. We saw friendships formed among the child's peer groups as well as friendships with adults outside of the family context. Not only were friends crucial in helping the children to gain a degree of independence from their families, but they also acted as shelters from the many storms of family life. The accounts of the 'traditional', Asian and transnational children show this quite clearly. Friends were also brought to the fore of family life by the children in split families, who explained how they relied on friendships to fulfil some of the functions normally undertaken by parents.

Family, Home and School

The accounts presented a picture of family, home and school as interconnected spheres in which the drama of the children's lives took place. The children's lives were not solely dominated by home and family. School figured largely with many of the children, who were unwilling to completely separate these influential life domains. Angel's reflections (transnational family) show just how critical a role school played in helping him to learn a new language and integrate into a new culture. The impact of school life and the values learned in the school environment provided him with much food for thought and helped him to recognize the advantages and disadvantages of life in both his original and newly adopted countries. In the case of Jonathan (traditional family) we can see how the home and family functions to support his educational progress in providing space, time and encouragement to succeed in school work.

Michele Moore, Judith Sixsmith and Kathleen Knowles

Unity in the Family

There were many instances in which the children talked about how their families pulled together to create a workable family unit. This sometimes involved sacrifices on the part of individual family members in the interests of the good of the family as a whole. Children offered parents practical support: doing the household chores; making breakfasts; and looking after siblings.

When working commitments were foremost for parents, the children were willing to help out in a variety of ways. For example, we see Meena (Asian family) helping out in the family business and the Bell child (multiple commitment family) taking responsibility for Aunt Polly. Children also offered emotional support to parents, brothers and sisters in times of stress and showed concern for their feelings, even in the delicacy with which they rendered their accounts. Regretfully, this can sometimes mean that they keep their problems out of parents' view and attempt to deal with them alone as they strive to protect their parents. The children in split families engaged in this tactic, as did children living in families with multiple commitments and the children in the transnational families.

Children Coping with Adversity

Perhaps one the most impressive aspects of the children's reflections is their ability to cope with adversity. Although sometimes it seemed that the children's difficulties extended beyond their ability to cope (see the following section), for the most part they were coping well in a wide variety of difficult and upsetting family experiences. Their accounts revealed the roots of their resilience. We saw, for example, how they drew on their personal strengths in coping with the practical and emotional problems of living in split families. The children's accounts of living in traditional families and in transnational families uncovered the ways in which they tapped into family support systems in order to deal with difficulties at school. A supportive family network was also very important to hearing children of d/Deaf parents when they were facing a hostile and discriminatory society. It seemed as if family cohesiveness increased through their mutual efforts to cope with adversity, perhaps best exemplified in Scott and Huw's (Hearing children of d/Deaf parents) caring and supportive attentions towards their mother.

However, as might be expected, children across different family types and at different stages in their lives did reveal difficulties in coping with their problems. In the next section, we consider some of the difficulties that children told us about, and make suggestions about how children can be helped to cope.

Helping Children and Their Families to Cope

All the children who talked to us had something to say about aspects of their home life that irritated, worried, upset or angered them. In many instances, the

138

children seemed to be drawing effectively on their personal resources that had built up over the course of their short lives, and were coping well with the difficulties. But others were struggling to manage problems. Let us take two brief examples: the Smith boy (multiple commitment family) was struggling with feelings of dislike towards his disabled sister; Jane (d/Deaf parents) was very worried about her brother's behaviour towards her deaf parents and upset at not being able to plan for her own independence. One reason that these cases merit attention is because they illustrate the importance, for parents and professionals alike, of recognizing pressures and stressors that children can be under which they might elect to conceal from the adults around them. In both these cases, the children felt unable to approach their parents with their concerns. In neither of these two cases was any professional support made available for these children.

For the Smith boy, the interview for this book was the first time that he had aired his feelings to an adult, an illuminating experience with beneficial results for him. In this case, the interview itself showed how listening to children can help them to reveal things to themselves and to think carefully about their taken-for-granted world. Jane, on the other hand, ended the interview in a tearful state and the interviewer afterwards wished perhaps that she had encouraged her to find ways forward and to identify people who could help her with her difficulties. (This point is taken up again in the third section of this chapter on methodological and ethical issues.)

Readers will have seen for themselves other examples in this book where there is a pressing need for helping children to identify coping strategies that go beyond the capabilities of individual family members (helping the 'trans-national' children to learn the language and integrate into their peer group, helping Meena and her Asian family to deal with the problem of conflicting cultural values, etc.). Children must be directly involved in evolving such strategies, otherwise much time and effort can be wasted in well-intentioned but misguided attempts by adults to produce solutions that children may find inappropriate. Parents, researchers, professionals and policy-makes must be prepared to ask children, — and listen to what they say, — about matters that directly involved children's well-being if they are to assert the right of children to have a voice in their own destinies.

It is not our intention here to attempt to enter into detailed recommendations for specific types of problematic family situations in which children find themselves. Instead, we should like to make a recommendation of a more general nature, related to the whole thrust of this book: we recommend that a holistic, individualized and child-centred perspective should be adopted when trying to understand the nature of a child's family life in any particular family, and when seeking to provide advice or support in difficult family situations. In doing so, we are not simply recycling old arguments on the dangers of viewing families as stereotypes, nor are we entering into political skirmishes about families. Neither would we like readers to think that by making such a general recommendation we are dodging the need to develop innovative ways to respond to children in the variety of difficult circumstances. To this end, it is hoped that the 'Thinking Points' sections will help readers to reflect on and reconceptualize their assumptions and practices. The 'Thinking Points' link what the children said to real issues for professionals and parents, so that the latter can 'reposition' and rethink how they react to, and deal with, children in families. This will go some way to assisting readers to adopt a child-centred perspective and begin to develop ways to empower individual children and their families to withstand adversity and cope with stress.

Methodological and Ethical Issues

The process of gathering information from the children has been a complex and demanding exercise. Throughout the chapters, authors have time and again referred to methodological and ethical problems with which they have been faced. At this point it is worth addressing some of these issues. We hope that by clarifying factors that might have influenced the children's accounts, readers may better understand the reflections themselves.

In many ways the accounts retold in this book are very much partial accounts. In no way do they represent a comprehensive picture of the children's family lives. Such partial accounts are a product of the research process. Most of us were strangers to the children. So they may have kept many secrets from us about their family. We asked the children about their private lives, and they chose what they wanted to divulge and what they preferred to keep hidden. In some instances the children specifically requested that we 'promise not to tell anyone' their most private revelations, particularly when they realized that their reflections raised issues about their personal loyalties. Where requested, we have omitted aspects of the children's stories which they told to us in confidence.

Furthermore, where the children's parents (or siblings) were present during the interview, their accounts may well have been compromised to some extent by their assessment of what they wanted their relatives to hear. This must be borne in mind when reading about the children living in split families, families with multiple commitments, dual career families and the hearing children with d/Deaf parents.

The issue of power relationships within the research process was a very important factor for us. As Griffin (1995) suggests, it is difficult to conduct any form of investigative process into which a degree of power differential between researcher and researched does not intrude. Where children are involved, the problem is magnified. Typically, in newly forged relationships, children often try to please and so defer to adults.

This is something we tried very hard to reduce to a minimum during our conversations with the children. We stressed that they were the experts on their own family experiences (Harre and Secord, 1972), that they were free to tell us what they wanted and that we were interested in whatever they had to say. It was also important to adopt an informal, friendly conversational style with the children, even to play with them in some instances, in order to minimize the formality of the interview situation which would place the burden of articulate, structured speech on the children. We hoped that in this way, the experience of the interview was transformed for the children into a special conversation over which they had much knowledge and some control. Even so, we acknowledge that they may at times have told us what they thought we wanted to hear, or they may have sought to provide what they thought were the 'right' answers to our questions.

Our relationships with the children were restricted (mainly to conversations), superficial and transitory. Had we known them for longer and in a different role relationship, we might well have revealed different and more diverse accounts of family life. Furthermore, the accounts we gathered were produced within the context of a particular encounter with a particular purpose behind it (Parker, 1992). The reflections the children gave must inevitably have varied according to their representations of their audience, as well as being influenced by their cultural, family and personal values (Henwood and Pidgeon, 1995).

The children's accounts also partly reproduce the constructed experiences of relationships, events and situations within the family. Their 'individual' stories are as much re-tellings of family constructions developed over time through shared membership of the family. From their position of insiders to their families, they have given us a public account of relationships, many of which may have been mutually constructed by the family itself.

We need to remember, too, that each child's reflections on their family life is only one perspective on that family. Beazley and Moore draw attention, in their chapter, to the fact that a very different picture of the families might have emerged had all the family members contributed to the research. Indeed Kagan and Lewis's chapter illustrates this very point, with each of the Green brothers in their multiple commitment family presenting very different portrayals of their family's life.

So, taken together, therefore, the effects of the interview situation, the selections children have made among their own experiences, the re-telling of family stories, and the focus on individual perspectives have all contributed to the partial nature of the children's reflections of family life reported in this book. This means that there are aspects of the children's stories which have not and, perhaps in some ways, cannot legitimately find their way into debates about family life.

Once the children's reflections were gathered, it was the researcher's task to structure the material in a way which made it available for the reader to understand. Each of us has pored over the transcripts of our conversations with the children and selected quotations which seemed to encapsulate the meaning of family life for the children. In presenting the material, we have elected to reproduce long quotations and extracts of conversations so that the reader can get a good feel for the context of the children's reflections.

Nevertheless, this process of selection and analysis has inevitably meant that a degree of researcher interpretation has unavoidably crept into the accounts. To guard against over-interpretation, where possible the children themselves have read the chapters and affirmed that the material in them is a reasonably accurate account of their family experiences. Having aired our concerns about the methodological and ethical limitations of our research, it is fair to say that such concerns are typical of most qualitative research (Gilbert, 1993; Homan, 1991; Shipman, 1988).

One additional and important point needs to be emphasized here. The children's reflections we have collected together are not meant to be representative of all children who live in similar family situations. Each child's family life is different. This book simply presents a glimpse of what it is like to live in these particular families from the perspective of the children. We hope that it encourages our readers to envisage a range of issues that children are meeting and dealing with. Since there are as many different accounts of the families as there are children interviewed, parents and professionals working with families need to recognize the danger of assuming that one's own personal view of a family represents a universal reality.

And finally, there was one ethical dimension to our work that we feel merits special attention. Readers will have seen that some contributors to this book came across children who were struggling with their problems. In such situations, the private lives of children present researchers with ethical dilemmas that can be very difficult to resolve. We had anticipated before we started the interviews that such situations might arise, and we held discussions on our position on giving advice and support to the children. Our discussions revolved around a number of questions and propositions that we reproduce here:

- The traditional role of researchers is to explore, investigate, report, but not intervene and change.

- We present ourselves to the children and their parents simply as researchers. We should therefore abide by this role.

- Circumstances may arise when to remain solely in the role of objective researcher would be an abandonment of ethical/moral responsibilities.

- If a serious problem is revealed and the child requests help/does not request help, is our duty to uphold confidentiality paramount or to actively engage in helping the child?

We have to admit that we did not come up with a clear-cut resolution. We concluded that each case had to be dealt with according to its particular circumstances, and each contributor had to decide for herself what to do if such an ethical dilemma presented itself. In fact, such dilemmas were not always resolved to the satisfaction of the contributors of this book, as readers will by now be aware.

Implications of Family-friendly Policies

Many of the children's parents were struggling to combine work and family life. Currently there is much debate about 'family-friendly policies' which aim to help parents and children cope with family and working life simultaneously. Family-friendly policies sometimes refer to employment or workplace practices, and sometimes to policies at the level of central government that purport to support the family (Cooper and Lewis, 1995). In this section we examine the implications of such policies in the light of issues and concerns that have emerged from this collection of children's accounts of their family lives. Our aim here is to demonstrate the importance of giving children a voice in decisions on matters that concern them, and to help open up future discussions that claim to be about improving family situations.

To start off with, some mention needs to be made of the scope of workplace family-friendly policies. These are usually based on narrow definitions of the family. Primarily these initiatives aim to help young mothers to combine work with the care of children, thus avoiding recruitment and workforce retention problems for the employers. It is suggested that few employers worry about being 'father-friendly' and suggest that at best such policies are 'traditional family-friendly' (Cooper and Lewis, 1995, p. 8). Such workplace initiatives that do not take into account the reality of British society, where families take increasingly diverse forms, seem exclusionary and ultimately their usefulness must be questioned.

Some family-friendly policies, such as career-break schemes and workplace nurseries, have been effective in reducing parental stress and helping parents to achieve a better balance between work and family time. Such policies and initiatives are not widespread or comprehensive enough. For example, the problems experienced by the children from the families with dual careers and multiple commitments demonstrate the need for additional support for these families. More family-friendly approaches at the workplace would go some way to relieving the children's difficulties which in many cases are closely related to the tensions between parents' work and family obligations.

Meanwhile, the 'friendliness' of other workplace initiatives does not bear close scrutiny. For example, how friendly to the family is the setting up of 24-hour crèches as currently exist in some towns and cities in the United States and Denmark, so that workers can do shifts without child-care problems? We would venture the opinion that this seems more like an 'employer-friendly' policy. And the implications of such practices for the children of these families are not known. Such very young children, of course, have no voice at all. The formulation and evaluation of these policies tend to focus on organizational rather than family consequences, and usually completely omit the perspectives of children and adolescents.

A case in point is the issue of relocation, which has been examined primarily by occupational psychologists. It is acknowledged that relocation, such as that experienced by the 'transnational' families in this book, can be stressful for children (Brett, Stroh and Reilly, 1992) but this tends to be ascertained from parents' reports, and it concerns employers mainly because of the impact it might have on parents' work performance. Employers (and many researchers) need to realize that children might see positive as well as negative consequences of such experiences and identify factors that could bring improvements to the situation. In ignoring the children's perspectives, both employers and the whole family lose out. On the one hand, children's stressful experiences simply continue without due attention. On the other hand, a potentially valuable contribution to the effectiveness of the policies is lost. We suggest that it could be cost effective and certainly more 'family-friendly' for organizations to consult with the children of their employees in the formulation, implementation and evaluation of family-friendly work initiatives.

Regarding policies at the level of central government, at present the situation in the United Kingdom, despite the rhetoric, is discouraging. In contrast to most other Member States in the European community, UK policies assume that the problem of reconciling work and family obligations is essentially a private matter that parents must resolve (Moss, 1996). Employment conditions and family situations in the UK are dictated by market forces and public spending considerations, not led by social policy. While these conditions prevail, we question the commitment of the United Kingdom to policies that support the family.

Policies that are truly aimed at supporting the family could improve not only the balance between work and home, but also improve children's and parents' experience of family life and minimize the problems that can occur in any family at any stage as they evolve and change over time. The pace of social and economic change in the United Kingdom is rapid and increasing. In common with writers such as Cooper and Lewis (1995), we feel there is an urgent need for wide-ranging discussions to develop a shared vision, not just of families, but of the sort of society that we would prefer to live in and the policies that are needed to achieve this. Most importantly, we believe it is imperative to place children's reflections firmly at the forefront of such dialogue. We urge parents, professionals and policy-makers to respect children's right to be heard.

Final Remarks

This book is primarily about children's reflections on family life and the children's reflections reported here are powerful enough to speak for themselves. We believe that the children's reflection must lead readers to challenge stereotypical assumptions often made about children in different family contexts. There are many lesson to be learned by listening to the children. We hope these lessons, through the medium of this book, will widen and stimulate discussion which will lead to the development of child- and family-friendly policy and practice.

Regarding UK policy and practice, some steps have been made towards recognizing children's rights by ratifying the 1991 UN Convention on the Rights of the Child. Unfortunately, the rights that are enshrined in this Convention, to civil liberties, to social provision and to protection, are not fully implemented in this country. It is essential that an independent body, for example a Children's Rights Commissioner, such as those that already exist in many other countries, be appointed in the UK to promote and monitor the full implementation of children's rights in the UK.

We affirm the need for children to be placed firmly in the driving seat when decisions are made that claim to be in their best interests and we are proud to have been able to give them a voice through the pages of this book. It is now a matter for parents, students of social science, professionals and practitioners with an interest in children's affairs to listen to what they have to say.

References

ABRAMOVITCH, A. and JOHNSON, L. (1992) 'Children's perceptions of parental work,' *Canadian Journal of Behavioural Science*, **24**, (3) pp. 329–32.

ALANEN, L. (1992) *Modern Childhood? Exploring the 'Child Question' in Sociology*, Institute for Educational Research Publication Series A, University of Jyvaskyla.

ALDRIDGE, J. and BECKER, S. (1993a) *Children Who Care — Inside the World of Young Carers*, Department of Social Sciences, Loughborough University / Nottingham Association of Voluntary Organisations.

ALDRIDGE, J. and BECKER, S. (1993b) *My Child, My Carer — The parents' Perspective*, Department of Social Sciences, Loughborough University / Nottingham Association of Voluntary Organisations.

ANWAR, M. (1981) *Between Two Cultures: A Story of the Relationships Between Generations in the Asian Community in Britain*, London, CRE.

BAKER, C. (1995) *A Parents' and Teachers' Guide to Bilingualism*, Clevedon, Multilingual Matters.

BALDWIN, S. (1985) *The Costs of Caring: Families With Disabled Children*, London, Routledge and Kegan Paul.

BALDWIN, S. and CARLISLE, J. (1994) *Social Support for Disabled Children and Their Families: A Review of the Literature*, Edinburgh, HMSO/SSI.

BALDWIN, S. and GLENDINNING, C. (1983) 'Employment, women and their disabled children,' in GROVES, D. and FINCH, J. (eds) *A Labour of Love: Women Work and Caring* London, Routledge and Kegan Paul.

BARNADOS TODAY (1994) *Facts About Families*, Issue 14, Spring/Summer.

BARNES, C. (1992) *Disabling Imagery and the Media: An Exploration of the Principles for Media Representations of Disabled People*, Halifax, Ryburn Publishing.

BEAZLEY, S. and MOORE, M. (1995) *Deaf Children, Their Families and Professionals: Dismantling Barriers*, London, David Fulton Publishers.

BEGUM, N. (1992a) *. . . Something To Be Proud Of . . . : The Lives of Asian Disabled People and Carers in Waltham Forest*, London, Waltham Forest Race Relations Unit.

BEGUM, N. (1992b) 'Doubly Disabled,' *Community Care Inside*, 24 September, pp. iii–iv.

BERESFORD, B. (1995) *Expert Opinions: A National Survey of Parents Caring for a Severely Disabled Child*, Bristol, Policy Press.

BOUVET, D. (1990) *The Path to Language: Bilingual Education for Deaf Children*, Clevedon, Multilingual Matters.

BOWMAN, B., BOWMAN, G. and RESCH, R. (1984) 'Humanizing the research interview,' *Quality and Quantity*, **18**, pp. 159–71.

BRANNEN, J., MESZAROS, P., MOSS, P. and POLAND, G. (1994) *Employment and Family Life. A Review of Research in the UK (1980–1994)*, London, Department of Employment.

BREAKWELL, G.M. (1986) *Coping with Threatened Identities*, London, Methuen.

BREAKWELL, G.M. (ed.) (1992) *Threatened Identities*, Chichester, John Wiley & Sons Ltd.

BRETT, J.M., STROH, L.K. and REILLY, A.H. (1992) 'What is it like being a dual career manager in the 1990s,' in ZEDECK, S. (ed.) *Work, Families and Organisations*, California, Jossey Bass.

BURMAN, E. (1994) *Deconstructing Developmental Psychology*, London, Routledge.

BURTON, M., KAGAN, C. with CLEMENTS, P. (1995) *Social Skills for People With Learning Disabilities: A Social Capability Approach*, London, Chapman and Hall.

CHILDREN'S RIGHTS OFFICE (1995) *Working Towards a Children's Rights Commissioner: News Update*, October, London.

COOPER, C. and LEWIS, S. (1995) *Beyond Family Friendly Organisations*, The Seven Million Project, Working Paper 2, London, DEMOS.

CORKER, M. (1993) Integration and deaf people,' in SWAIN, J., FINKELSTEIN, V., FRENCH, S. and OLIVER, M. (eds) *Disabling Barriers — Enabling Environments*, London, Sage.

CORKER, M. (1996) 'Hearing difficulty as impairment,' in HALES, G. (ed.) *Beyond Disability: Towards an Enabling Society*, London, Sage.

CORSON, D. (1993) *Language, Minority Education and Gender: Linking Social Justice and Power*, Clevedon, Multilingual Matters.

CRONIN, O. (1993) 'Helping children to recall: Reading 5,' in Open University Resources Booklet K501, *Investigative Interviewing with Children*, Milton Keynes, The Open University.

DEMO, D. and ACOCK, A. (1993) 'Family diversity and the division of domestic labour: How much have things really changed?' *Family Relations*, **42** (3), pp. 323–31.

DENZIN, N. and LINCOLN, Y. (eds) (1994) *Handbook of Qualitative Research*, London, Sage.

DEPARTMENT OF THE ENVIRONMENT (1996) *Housing Bill: Allocation of Housing Accommodation by Local Authorities: A Consultation Paper*, Department of the Environment, London.

DEPRES, C. (1991) 'The meaning of home: Literature review and directions for future research and theoretical development,' *Journal of Architectural and Planning Research*, **8** (2), pp. 96–115.

DILWORTH-ANDERSON, P., BURTON, L. and TURNER, W. (1993) 'The importance of values in the study of culturally diverse families,' *Family Relations*, **42** (3), pp. 238–42.

DRURY, B. (1991) 'Sikh girls and the maintenance of an ethnic culture,' *New Community*, **17** (3), pp. 387–99, April.

FINCH, J. and MASON, J. (1993) *Negotiating Family Responsibilities*, London, Routledge.

FINE, M. (1993) 'Current approaches to understanding family diversity,' *Family Relations*, **42** (3), pp. 235–7.

FRANKILIN, B. (1986) 'Children's political rights,' in FRANKLIN, B. (ed.) *The Rights of Children*, Oxford, Blackwell.

FRANKLIN, B. (1995) *The Handbook of Children's Rights: Comparative Policy and Practice*, London, Routledge.

FURNHAM, A. and BOCHNER, S. (1986) *Culture Shock: Psychological Reactions of Unfamiliar Environments*, London, Methuen.

GILBERT, L.A. and DANCER, L.S. (1992) 'Dual earner families in the United States and adolescent development,' in LEWIS, S., IZRAELI, D.N. and HOOTSMANS, H. (eds) *Dual Earner Families: International Perspectives*, London, Sage.

GILBERT, N. (ed.) (1993) *Researching Social Life*, London, Sage.

GOLDSCHEIDER, F. and WAITE, L. (1991) *New Families, No Families? The Transformation of the American Home*, Berkeley, University of California Press.

GRAHAM, H. (1993) *Hardship and Health in Women's Lives*, London, Harvester Wheatsheaf.

GREGORY, S. and HARTLEY, G. (eds) (1991) *Constructing Deafness*, London, Pinter.

GREGORY, S., WELLS, A. and SMITH, S. (1996) *Bilingual Education with Deaf Children*, Clevedon, Multilingual Matters.

GRIFFIN, C. (1995) 'Feminism, social psychology and qualitative research,' *The Psychologist*, **8** (3), pp. 119–21.

HAMMERSLEY, M. and ATKINSON, P. (1983) *Ethnography: Principles in Practice*, London, Tavistock.

HARRE, R. and SECORD, P. (1972) *The Explanation of Social Behaviour*, Oxford, Blackwell.

HAYWARD, G. (1977) 'Psychological Concepts of Home from Urban Middle Class Families.' Unpublished PhD Thesis, CUNY.

HENWOOD, K. and NICHOLSON, P. (1995) 'Qualitative research,' *The Psychologist*, **8** (3), pp. 109–10.

HENWOOD, K. and PIDGEON, N. (1995) 'Grounded theory and psychological research,' *The Psychologist*, **8** (3), pp. 115–18.

HMSO (1989) *The Children Act*, London, HMSO.

HOCHSCHILD, A. (1989) *Second Shift: Working Parents and the Revolution in the Home*, New York, Viking Penguin.

HOFFMAN, L. (1989) 'Effects of maternal employment in the two parent family,' *American Psychologist*, **44**, pp. 283–92.

HOMAN, R. (1991) *The Ethics of Social Research*, London, Longman.

INGLEBY, D. (1986) 'Development in social context,' in RICHARDS, M. and LIGHT, P. (eds) *children of Social Worlds*, Cambridge, Polity Press.

JAMES, A. and PROUT, J. (eds) (1990) *Constructing and Reconstructing Childhood*, London, Falmer Press.

KAGAN, K. and LEWIS, S. (1995) *Family, Employment and Social Change in Britain: Accounts of Women with Multiple Commitments*, IOD Occasional Paper 1/95, Manchester, IOD Research Group.

KEITH, L. (ed.) (1994) *Mustn't Grumble*, London, The Women's Press.

KENYON, D. (1994) 'Reaction–Interaction,' in KEITH L. (ed.) (1994) *Mustn't Grumble*, London, The Women's Press.

KITWOOD, T. (1983) *Self-conception Among Young British Asian Muslims: Confrontation of a Stereotype*, Chichester, John Wiley & Sons Ltd.

LAWRENCE, R. (1991) 'The meaning and use of home,' *Journal of Architectural and Planning Research*, **8** (2), pp. 91–5.

LEACH, P. (1994) *Children First*, Harmondsworth, Penguin.

LEWIS, S., IZRAELI, D.N. and HOOTSMANS, H. (1992) *Dual Career Families: International Perspectives*, London; Sage.

LEWIS, S. and COOPER, C.L. (1987) 'Stress in dual earner couples and stage in the life cycle,' *Journal of Occupational Psychology*, **60**, pp. 289–303.

LEWIS, S. and COOPER, C.L. (1988) 'Stress in dual-earner families,' in GUTEK, B.A., STROMBERG, A.H. and LARWOOD, L. (eds) *Women and Work: An Annual Review*, Volume 3. Newbury Park; Sage.

LEWIS, S. and COOPER, C. (1989) *Career Couples*, London, Unwin Hyman.

LEWIS, S. and KNOWLES, K. (1995) 'Family consequences of dual career partnerships.' Conference paper presented at the conference on Estres en Nions y Adolescentes, University of Murcia, November.

LEWIS, S. and TAYLOR, K. (in press) 'Evaluating the impact of family friendly employer policies: A case study,' in LEWIS, S. and LEWIS, J. (eds) *The Work Family Challenge: Rethinking Employment,* London, Sage.

MACASKILL, C. (1985) 'The Verdict of Siblings,' in *Against the Odds: Adopting Mentally Handicapped Children*, London, British Agencies for Adoption and Fostering.

MASON, M. (1995) 'Inclusion: Empowering Disabled People.' Paper presented at the Conference on the UN Convention on the Rights of the Child, UN Rules on Disabled People and UNESCO Statement on Inclusive Education, December, London, Centre for Studies on Inclusive Education.

McEWEN, K. and BARLING, J. (1993) 'Effects of maternal employment experiences on children's behaviour, mood and cognitive functioning,' *Journal of Marriage and the Family*, **53**, pp. 635–44.

MODGIL, S. (1986) *Multicultural Education: The Interminable Debate*, London, Falmer Press.

MOORE, M., BEAZLEY, S. and MAELZER, J. (forthcoming) *Researching Disability Issues*, Milton Keynes, Open University Press.

MOORE, M., BEAZLEY, S. and MAELZER, J. (forthcoming) *Enabling Disabled Parents*, London, David Fulton Publishers.

MORRIS, J. (1991) *Pride Against Prejudice: Transforming Attitudes of Disability*, London, The Women's Press.

MORRIS, J. (ed.) (1992) *Alone Together: Voices of Single Mothers*, London, The Women's Press.

MORRIS, J. (1993) *Independent Lives? Community Care and Disabled People*, Basingstoke, Macmillan.

MOSS, P. (1996) 'Reconciling employment and family responsibilities: A European perspective,' in LEWIS, S. and LEWIS, J. (eds) *The Work Family Challenge: Rethinking Employment*, London, Sage.

NEWELL, P. (1995) 'The Case for an End to Segregated Education.' Paper presented at the Conference on the UN Convention on the rights of the Child, UN Rules on Disabled People and UNESCO Statement on Inclusive Education December, London, Centre for Studies on Inclusive Education.

Observer (1993) 'Editorial column,' 17 October.

OLIVER, M. (1990) *The Politics of Disablement*, London, Macmillan.

OLIVER, M. (1996) *Understanding Disability: From Theory to Practice*, London, Macmillan.

OLSEN, R. (1996) 'Young carers: Challenging the facts and politics of research into children and caring,' *Disability and Society*, **11** (1), pp. 41–54.

PARKER, G. (1990) *With Due Care and Attention* (2nd edn), London, Family Policy Studies Centre.

PARKER, I. (1992) *Discourse Dynamics: Critical Analysis for Social and Individual Psychology*, London, Routledge.

PIPER, C. (1994) 'Parental authority and the Education Act,' *Family Law*, **24** (March), pp. 146–9.

PRESTON, P. (1994) *Mother Father Deaf*, London, Harvester Wheatsheaf.

PRIESTLEY, M. (1995) 'Commonality and difference in the movement: An "Association of Blind Asians" in Leeds,' *Disability and Society*, **10** (June) (2), pp. 157–69.

RANA, B. (1995) 'The Experiences of Second Generation Sikh Women Living in Britain.' Unpublished Undergraduate Thesis, Manchester Metropolitan University.

RICHARDS, L. and SCHMIEGE, C. (1993) 'Problems and strengths of single parent families,' *Family Relations*, **42** (3), pp. 277–85.

ROBINSON, K. (1995) 'Book review,' *British Deaf News*, **26** (12), p. 17.

ROUT, U. and ROUT, J. (1993) *Stress and General Practitioners*, London, Kluwer.

RUTTER, M. and RUTTER, M. (1992) *Developing Minds: Challenge and Continuity Across the Life Span*, Harmondsworth, Penguin.

SEGAL, J. and SIMKINS, J. (1993) *My Mum Needs Me: Helping Children with Ill or Disabled Parents*, Harmondsworth, Penguin.

SHAH, R. (1992) *The Silent Minority: Children with Disabilities in Asian Families*, London, National Children's Bureau.

SHAKESPEARE, P., ATKINSON, D. and FRENCH, S. (1993) *Reflecting on Research Practice: Issues in Health and Social Welfare*, Milton Keynes, Open University Press.

SHIPMAN, M. (1988) *The Limitations of Social Research*, London, Longman.

SIXSMITH, A. and SIXSMITH, J. (1991) 'Transitions in home experience in later life,' *Journal of Architectural and Planning Research*, **8** (3).

SIXSMITH, J. (1986) 'The meaning of home: An exploratory study of environmental experience,' *Journal of Environmental Psychology*, **6**, pp. 281–98.

SIXSMITH, J. and SIXSMITH, A. (1990) 'Places in transition: The impact of life events on the experience of home,' in PUTNAMO, T. and NEWTON, C. (eds) *Household Choices*, London, Futures Publications.

SOLBERG, A. (1990) 'Negotiating childhood: Changing constructions of age for Norwegian children,' in JAMES, A. and PROUT, J. (eds) *Constructing and Reconstructing Childhood*, London, Falmer Press.

STOPES-ROE, M. and COCHRANE, R. (1990) 'The child-rearing values of Asian and British parents and young people: An inter-ethnic and inter-generational comparison in the evaluation of Kohn's 13 qualities,' *British Journal of Social Psychology*, **29**, pp. 149–60.

TUNSTILL, J., ALDGATE, J., WILSON, M. and SUTTON, P. (1996) 'Crossing the organisational divide: Family support services,' *Health and Social Care in the Community*, **4** (1), pp. 41–9.

UNICEF (1995) *The Convention on the Rights of the Child*, UNICEF.

VAN DER KLIFT, E. and KUNC, N. (1994) 'Hell-bent on helping: Benevolence, friendship and the politics of help,' in THOUSAND, J., VILLA, R. and NEVIN, A. (eds) *Creativity and Collaborative Learning: A Practical Guide to Empowering Students and Teachers*, Baltimore, Paul Brooks.

WADE, B. and SOUTER, P. (1992) *Continuing to Think: The British Asian Girl. An exploratory study of the influence of culture upon a group of British Asian girls with specific reference to the teaching of English*, Clevedon, Multilingual Matters.

WALLERSTEIN, J.S. and BLAKESLEE, S. (1989) *Second Chances: Men, Women and Children a Decade After Divorce*, New York, Tickner and Fields.

WESTWOOD, S. and BHACHU, P. (1988) *Enterprising Women, Ethnicity, Economy and Gender Relations*, London, Routledge.

WHITE, D. and WOOLLETT, A. (1992) *Families: A Context for Development*, London, Falmer Press.

WHITHEAD, B. (1993) 'Dan Quayle Was Right,' *The Atlantic*, April, pp. 47–84.

WINNICOTT, D. (1964) *The Child, The Family and The Outside World*, Harmondsworth, Penguin.

WOOLLETT, A. (1986) 'The influence of older siblings on the language environment of younger children,' *British Journal of Developmental Psychology*, **4**, pp. 235–45.

ZIRINSKY, L. (1994) 'Brothers and sisters,' in HILL, L. (ed.) *Caring for Dying Children and Their Families*, London, Chapman and Hall.

Notes on Contributors

All of the contributors lecture in the Department of Psychology and Speech Pathology at the Manchester Metropolitan University. They have published widely in their respective specialist areas, and their work is well known both nationally and internationally. Areas of expertise are as follows:

Sarah Beazley is a Specialist Speech and Language Therapist for Deaf People who carries out freelance clinical and consultancy work. She is involved with other therapists in a Communication Skills Development Group providing training in the field. She has written widely about her work on language and communication development and is currently co-writing two books on disability matters.

Dr Carolyn Kagan is a Principal Lecturer with wide-ranging experience in the area of interpersonal and organizational development and change. She is currently a joint grant holder with Dr Suzan Lewis for a project on families combining work and caring for disabled children funded by the Joseph Rowntree Foundation. She is co-author of *Social Skills for People with Learning Disabilities: A Social Capability Approach* (1995).

Kathleen Knowles is involved in a variety of European initiatives in community psychology, such as programmes for the rehabilitation of people experiencing long-term disability, including chronic mental illness. Her specialist interests are psycho-social rehabilitation in the community and independent living for adults with chronic mental illness. She is co-editing a book on independent living in the community and is a member of the advisory committee for the Spanish journal *Psychosocial Rehabilitation With and Within the Community*.

Dr Suzan Lewis has written extensively on the far-reaching implications of the dual career family. Recent publications include *Dual Career Families: International Perspectives* (1992) of which she is co-editor and *The Work Family Challenge: Rethinking Employment* (forthcoming). She increasingly informs national and international policy on reconciliation between work and home obligations.

Dr Michele Moore runs a postgraduate programme in Psychology and Disability Studies which is currently unique in the United Kingdom. She is a Reviews Editor for the journal *Disability and Society*, and involved in research on disabled parenting, family life and independent living. She is co-author of several books in the field, together with Sarah Beazley and June Maelzer.

Dr Usha Rout specializes in the areas of social and organizational psychology. Her current research interests include stress encountered by primary health-care professionals and their families, the diagnosis of depression in primary care settings and the experience of Asian women working in America, Britain and India. She has published widely on these topics.

Dr Judith Sixsmith is a social psychologist whose work on environmental issues, quality of life and ageing reaches an extensive national and international audience. She is co-author of a forthcoming book on older people and TV watching (University of Liverpool Press). She is a Consultant Evaluator for the European Community Framework 4 Technological Innovations for the Disabled and Elderly initiative. Currently she is a Consultant Editor for the *Journal of Environmental Psychology.*

Index

Index